ASTONISHING
X-MEN

GIFTED

**BASED ON THE COMIC SERIES
BY JOSS WHEDON AND JOHN CASSADAY**

ASTONISHING X-MEN: GIFTED PROSE NOVEL. Published by MARVEL WORLDWIDE, INC., a subsidiary of MARVEL ENTERTAINMENT, LLC. OFFICE OF PUBLICATION: 135 West 50th Street, New York, NY, 10020. Copyright © 2013 Marvel Characters, Inc. All rights reserved.

ISBN# 978-0-7851-6515-6.

Printed in the U.S.A.

ALAN FINE, EVP - Office of the President, Marvel Worldwide, Inc. and EVP & CMO Marvel Characters B.V.; DAN BUCKLEY, Publisher & President - Print, Animation & Digital Divisions; JOE QUESADA, Chief Creative Officer; TOM BREVOORT, SVP of Publishing; DAVID BOGART, SVP of Operations & Procurement, Publishing; C.B. CEBULSKI, SVP of Creator & Content Development; DAVID GABRIEL, SVP of Print & Digital Publishing Sales; JIM O'KEEFE, VP of Operations & Logistics; DAN CARR, Executive Director of Publishing Technology; SUSAN CRESPI, Editorial Operations Manager; ALEX MORALES, Publishing Operations Manager; STAN LEE, Chairman Emeritus. For information regarding advertising in Marvel Comics or on Marvel.com, please contact Niza Disla, Director of Marvel Partnerships, at ndisla@marvel.com. For Marvel subscription inquiries, please call 800-217-9158. Manufactured between 4/17/13 and 5/20/13 by SHERIDAN BOOKS, INC., CHELSEA, MI, USA.

First printing 2013
10 9 8 7 6 5 4 3 2 1

Cover and Interior Art by John Cassaday

Stuart Moore, Editor

Design by Spring Hoteling

Senior Editor, Special Projects: Jeff Youngquist

SVP of Print & Digital Publishing Sales: David Gabriel

Editor in Chief: Axel Alonso

Chief Creative Officer: Joe Quesada

Publisher: Dan Buckley

Executive Producer: Alan Fine

To Axel for thinking of me,
Stuart for guiding me through,
and Joss for being astonishing.

ASTONISHING
X-MEN
GIFTED

A NOVEL OF THE MARVEL UNIVERSE

I'm all alone.

I can feel my heart pounding in my chest, and part of me wants to run home screaming to my parents. I'm thirteen years old. Well, thirteen and a half. Worse, I'm the age where "and a half" actually means something, like it's a point of pride because you're six months closer to hitting the age of consent in four more years and the drinking age three years after that. Anyway, the point is: thirteen. And a half. Someone who's thirteen and a half shouldn't have to be dealing with things like this, things my parents would be helpless to do anything about.

I mean, what the hell would I say to them? "Mom, Dad…the X-Men have been captured. Any thoughts?"

It's a horrifying situation to be in, knowing that I'm so far beyond their ability to counsel me or give me advice or help me in any way. This can't be made better with a plate of fresh-baked cookies and cold milk while my father assures me that the other girls are just jealous of me, and my mother says I should be proud of my damned hair that defies even the most dedicated hairdresser's efforts to straighten it out. All those pleasant bromides, all those as-

surances, don't mean a thing in the face of…oh, right…
THE X-MEN, THE GREATEST TEAM OF MUTANT HEROES
EVER, HAVE BEEN CAPTURED. And I'm the only one who
can do anything about it.

It's not fair that all this is getting dumped on my shoulders. Who am I? Katherine Pryde, teenage big-brain, who
usually wears her Mogen David around her throat and her
heart on her sleeve.

I'm in the hold of a small hovercraft that's barreling
down some random street in New York, which shows you
just how screwed up my life has become, because when
was the last time you saw a hovercraft buzzing along in
Manhattan? The bad guys are in the front section of the
ship. I can't see them. I can hear them talking about their
plans, but only in broad strokes. None of it makes any
sense.

Then I hear my name. Some goon is asking about me.
Some woman is responding. Her voice is familiar.

I decide I have to take the chance and see what's going on.

I put my hand tentatively against the bulkhead, and then
ease my molecules into it. I'm able to pass through it entirely,
like a ghost. I hold my breath because I don't know what would
happen if I tried to inhale inside a wall. It makes me feel tingly
as I phase through the wall and emerge on the other side.

And I see the woman. Her back is to me, but I'd know
her anywhere.

It's that Miss Frost woman. The one who was head of
that other Academy my parents wanted me to go to before

they decided I'd go to the one run by Professor Charles Xavier. This woman, this Emma Frost, who looked me straight in the eye and told me that we were going to be great friends.

And what the hell is she wearing? Panties, thigh-boots, a corset and a cape, all in white? Who's flying this ship? Hugh Hefner?

Emma Frost and her goon squad are holding the X-Men prisoners. I gotta help 'em. But how? These guys have guns and super-powers, and I'm just me.

I wait. I wait for my moment, and suddenly I'm making my move. We're not in the ship. When did we leave the ship? I don't know, but suddenly I'm in a building, and the X-Men are in cages. I move through a wall, and there's one of the X-Men—Storm, the weather witch—drugged up and in a cage. I go to her and suddenly she's telling me to get away, and oh my God, it's Emma Frost, she sees me and she's sending her goons after me. I run, my heart throbbing, and I dive headlong into the floor as Frost screams behind me, "Seal the complex! Organize search teams! I want Kitty Pryde found at once!" I've never heard such pure evil, such vindictiveness, and I know she's going to do terrible things to me.

And then I'm out of the building, sprinting down an alleyway. It's so cold, and I'm only wearing jeans, a tube top and a light vest. I'm shivering with both chill and terror, and suddenly lights illuminate the alleyway behind me. It's a car bearing down on me, and I'm running and I can't see, I can't concentrate, I'm just too terrified. I stumble. I fall. My mind is scattered. Instead of phasing through the ground, my arm hits hard.

There's no pain. I don't know why. I feel like there should be.

There's nothing in my field of vision except cascading waves of light from the car's headlights, getting brighter and brighter. I try to scream. I want to desperately. It's stalled in my chest, and I'm physically forcing it up, up to my throat and then out, first small and strangled and finally out—

And I sit up, jolted awake by my own scream as it hauls me into the waking world. Instantly I clamp my hands over my mouth, terrified that I might have been loud enough to disturb my parents. It was so nice of them to let me crash in my old room here in Deerfield while I'm between apartments; the last thing I want to do is repay their kindness by disturbing them in the night.

I hear nothing. Bullet dodged.

I click on the lamp that's sitting on the nightstand and squint against the illumination. It's three in the morning. My room is a memorial to the person I used to be, the walls festooned with posters of boy bands that once meant the world to me. Back when my world was easy. Back when my world made sense.

The letter is still on the nightstand. Crisp white paper, neatly folded in threes. It should be a small wadded ball, or torn to shreds. That's what I should have done with it. But no, the letter just sits there, taunting me. I should have ripped it up, yet there it sits, like a zit on prom night. If I had destroyed it, then knowing its author, knowing her, another one would simply have shown up, and another, and then hundreds more, blowing through the windows and down the chimney like in *Harry Potter*, filling the living room with nothing but her, that witch.

I take a moment to reflect on my dreams. For most people, nightmares are random, deep-seated thoughts and fears that seep from your subconscious into your sleeping mind and toss you into the midst of impossible worst-case scenarios. What does it say about my life that everything I just dreamt about actually happened to me, beat for beat, note for note? All of those emotions, all of those horrifying first encounters, as fresh and real to me as when I first experienced them years ago. Unfiltered, unchanged, un-dimmed by the passage of time.

I thought I'd left them all behind. After all, in my "career," I've gone on to experience far worse nights than that one. I've experienced heartbreaking loss.

There was Jean Grey, the red-haired heroine who was probably the most powerful telekinetic force on Earth…the woman who actually saved me that night from the guys chasing me in the alleyway…beloved of the X-Men's leader, Scott Summers…

Dead.

There was Peter Rasputin—Colossus—the metal-covered Russian farm boy, impenetrable on the outside, sweet and easily wounded on the inside...beloved of... me...

Dead.

And others, too.

I remember when I was twelve, and Joey Reisman got hit and killed by a car while he was crossing the street going to a deli. I had a crush on him at the time and I cried for weeks. Literally. For weeks. Death seemed unimaginable to me.

Now it's called a day at the office.

I've left the office. I've left the X-Men.

Yet the letter sits there, taunting me.

The letter from her. Miss "We're going to be great friends."

I pick it up with the intention of finally crumpling it and freeing myself from her, once and for all. The letterhead, lightly embossed in simple black letters that do nothing to convey what "Professor Xavier's School for Gifted Young-sters" really means.

"Dear Kitty"

An overly obvious endeavor to be friendly. Like we're even remotely friends.

"Dear Kitty: With the new semester beginning, it is our belief"

Our? Yours and who else's? Scott, who's now your boyfriend, and what the hell is up with that? Or did the whole group vote on it? Or is it just you, writing with the imperial "we" like the queen bee-yotch that you are?

"that you would make a valuable addition to the faculty.

Your responsibilities would include"

The letter is less than half a page. It says what my duties would be, tells me the starting salary—fixed, no negotiation—plus medical and, hey, dental. I'd really need that considering my teeth are already on edge just from the thought of dealing with her.

It concludes:

"Please feel free to call my private number, provided below, during normal business hours."

I check the number against a keypad to see if by some chance the digits correspond to 914-SKANKHO. Sadly they don't.

That's all there is to the letter. No apology for past wrongs. No attempt at explanations. Once she was evil, now she's good, and we're all just supposed to accept that and move on.

I can't.

We're supposed to trust her.

I don't.

"Hello, Katherine. I'm sure we're going to be great friends."

Her first words to me. I can still see her, standing there in my parents' living room, with her underwear actually under her wear. That viper smile, those cold eyes. I could see right through her...

No, you couldn't.

I'm busted by my own mind.

The truth is, I couldn't see through her. She seemed a

little creepy, kind of standoffish. But she didn't radiate evil. I had no idea the kind of stuff she was really into. No clue how truly and utterly dangerous she was. How could I have? How could anyone?

Especially kids.

All those kids, all those young mutants in the Xavier School, looking to her for guidance, for information, for the facts of mutant life. And the others were letting her do it. Scott Summers, a.k.a. Cyclops. Hank McCoy, the Beast, one of the smartest men I've ever known. Logan—Wolverine—who could literally smell a threat from a hundred yards away: Why hadn't he just gutted her and moved on? Why were such savvy people letting Emma Frost within a mile of easily influenced youngsters? Were they just willing to hand her an entire new generation of potentially evil mutants? Did people not understand what that meant anymore?

Guess not. It's all about branding these days. Even the evil mutants don't call themselves evil anymore. And people buy into it. If Magneto called his followers "The Legion of Happy Fun Guys," they'd probably have people lining up out the door.

The school was part of my past. I'd moved on.

And so had Emma Frost. But now she's moved on to my former territory, molding and shaping a class of young "me's." And I'm supposed to…what? Stand by and let it happen?

It wasn't my problem.

I was finished.

I was done.

Done.

Donne.

John Donne.

British poet, lived during the mid-1600s.

No man is an island entire of itself; every man is a piece of the continent, a part of the main; if a clod be washed away by the sea, Europe is the less, as well as if a promontory were, as well as a manor of thy friends or of thine own were; any man's death diminishes me, because I am involved in mankind. And therefore never send to know for whom the bell tolls; it tolls for thee.

I hate the way my mind works, especially when it starts free-form associating.

The school bell is tolling, and even if I don't go there, it's tolling for me because we're all mutants, all mutantkind, and what happens with mutantkind is also going to happen to me. We're all connected. And if Emma Frost manages to undermine the values of the Xavier School, it's going to wind up biting us all on the ass. And I'm part of "all" no matter how much I want it otherwise.

My grandmother had a saying: One choice is no choice.

I glance at the clock again. The numbers 3:03 glow in red.

Maybe I can wake her up. If I'm going to be rousted from a sound sleep because of her, the least I can do is extend her the same courtesy.

I pick up my cell phone and dial her personal number.

My phone has a privacy block on it; she won't know it's me until she hears my voice waking her up.

She picks it up on the second ring. There is no trace of slumber in her voice; she's fully awake.

"Hello, Katherine," she says crisply. *"I was expecting your call."*

God, I hate her.

ONE

---⟡---

"GENTLEMEN...I cannot believe you're serious."

Doctor Kavita Rao was sitting in a conference room, staring at an impassive array of bean counters seated across from her. She wanted to lunge across the round mahogany table, grab the nearest man by his pressed, starched shirt, and give him a good shaking. Rao prided herself on her professional demeanor, however, so that was never really an option, no matter how much pleasure she would have taken in it.

She was a slender woman, her dark skin, delicate features and red Bindi mark on her forehead conveying her Indian origins. Her black hair was tied back, adding to her all-business look, and she peered over the tops of her rectangular spectacles in the way she typically did when she was incredulous about something.

"I'm afraid, Doctor Rao, that we have no choice," said one of the bean counters. It didn't matter to her which one it was; they were all the same as far as she was concerned. "This was not an easy decision to make…"

"This should not be *your* decision to make at all." Her lips were thinned practically to invisibility. "None of you are scientists."

"Quite true," said another bean counter. "And that is precisely why Benetech depends upon us."

"I'm not sure I follow, Mister…?"

"Bean," he said.

She blinked and the edges of her mouth nearly twitched, betraying amusement. "Seriously?"

"Yes. Why?" He stared at her in puzzlement. "Is there a problem?"

Immediately, she got herself back under control. "Yes, there's a problem," she said curtly. "You're talking about gutting my department."

"We're talking about reapportioning staff and trimming back unnecessary expenditure—"

"Excuse me, Mister Bean, but I prefer to use one word rather than fifty. You can rattle on as long as you wish, but 'gutting' seems the succinct way to describe what you're proposing."

"Fine," said Mr. Bean with a shrug. "You can use whatever terminology you wish…"

"Thanks *ever* so…"

"But the bottom line is that the board has asked for our recommendations as to what departments could be scaled back and, unfortunately, the research in which you've been engaging seems…what's the best word—?"

"Limited?" suggested one of the other accountants.

"Yes, exactly, limited," said Mr. Bean, his head bobbing. "That's a good word."

"No, it's a wrong word. There is nothing limited about our research…"

"Yes, there is," said Mr. Bean firmly. "First of all, it caters to the needs of a very small percentage of the population. Relatively speaking, a minuscule portion…"

"Nonsense," she said brusquely. "There are other genetic conditions, deformities, that Benetech is researching, that are far rarer—not to mention less potentially destructive—than what I've been investigating."

"Yes, but you've been investigating it for years, and apparently you're no closer to a solution than you were when you started." He sounded sympathetic rather than harsh, but the words still hit like body blows. "Am I correct?"

"These things take time."

"I'm sure they do, but that doesn't answer the question. Am I correct?"

She tapped a finger on the table, a nervous habit that she was unable to quit no matter how hard she tried. It grated on her to admit it, but she had to: "That would be a fair assessment."

"Well...there you have it," said Mr. Bean. He had a thick folder open in front of him and when he closed it, it was like the gates of hell slamming shut. "Understand that we are informing you of our recommendation purely as a courtesy—"

"What are you not saying?" she demanded, her eyes narrowing.

Mr. Bean looked politely confused. "I'm not sure I—"

"There's something else. Something you're not telling me. I'm very good at reading body language, Mr. Bean, and there's something going on that you're not being candid about."

He exchanged glances with the others of his ilk at the table, and then he cleared his throat and said, "The, uh...the simple fact, Doctor Rao, is that mutants aren't what one might call sexy."

She stared at him as if he'd suddenly started speaking in tongues. "I'm sorry? Not...sexy? Have you *seen* some of their outfits?"

Mr. Bean and the others started to laugh until they saw that she wasn't, at which point they immediately fell silent.

"What I mean to say is that mutantcy isn't like,

say, sickle-cell or Tay-Sachs or Parkinson's. It doesn't have someone like Michael J. Fox who everybody adores going around filming commercials or testifying to Congress about how funds are needed for research. People are, in fact, terrified of mutants. Even the so called,"—he held up finger quotes—"'good mutants' are objects of fear, because you never know when they're going to turn evil or destroy property fighting the mutants that supposedly are worse than they are. You think the average citizen cares about who's good and who's evil in one of these huge fights? They don't. To them, it's an extended bar brawl that's spilled out into their front yards and demolished their new Ford Fusions."

"You're telling me," she said slowly, "that despite the fact that people are suffering—both mutants and average citizens. Benetech won't support research into mutants because they can't use it for *fundraising?*"

"Sad to say, yes. That's exactly right. Especially when it's combined with the lack of progress. It's not like muscular dystrophy where telethons can be held for decades, and people understand the fact that the condition is still around. Being a mutant is simply a different proposition from other genetic research. And that's the truth."

"Really." She stood up, knowing there was no point in continuing the discussion. That indeed there hadn't actually been a discussion. The men automatically rose when she did. Then she ticked off on her fingers, one at a time: "Muscular dystrophy. Cystic fibrosis. Hemophilia. Tay-Sachs. Sickle-cell. Do you know what all of those are?"

"Diseases?" said Mr. Bean, looking puzzled.

"Mutations. Every single one. Point mutations, to be specific. And people treat those sufferers with simple human compassion. If we'd spent all this time trying to help mutants instead of running from them or attacking them, then maybe—just maybe—the research would be further along."

"Well," and he shrugged, "I guess we'll never know, will we?"

"No," she said icily. "We won't."

She walked out without another word.

RAO strode down the hallway, the edges of the lab coat, worn over her sari, swirling around her legs. Her fists were clenched tightly and her posture was ramrod straight.

Fools. Blind fools. They don't understand. None of them understand.

She wondered how much of her department was going to be left when she returned to it. Would her office even be there? Maybe they were just planning to move her desk into the cafeteria. She could continue to do her work as long as she was willing to bus tables.

Then, as she walked past one lab that had been emptied during the last round of budget cuts, she heard a deep, rough voice call to her from within. "Doctor Rao," it said.

She turned and looked. The main light wasn't on, but the glow from a single overhead fixture provided some illumination. Rao stepped to the threshold and looked inside.

There was a table in the middle of the room with various papers and file folders on it, arranged in what appeared to be a rather haphazard fashion. Even from this distance, though, she could discern that the materials involved genetic research.

Otherwise the room was filled with shadows. She thought she could make out someone at the far end. Someone big, built like a linebacker. Beyond his general shape, though, she couldn't see any details.

"Come in, please, Doctor Rao," said the voice. It was deep, sonorous, but otherwise didn't sound particularly threatening. "Close the door behind you."

She automatically reached over and flipped the main light switch. It clicked impotently.

Well, this *is coming across like a bad horror movie.*

"As an alternative proposal," she said, still not stepping inside, "how about I call security?"

"By the time they arrive, I'll be gone," said the voice. "Along with all that tasty research on the table—which, I have reason to believe, will be of great interest to you."

On a day that was already spectacularly bad, she wondered pragmatically if it could really get any worse. So what if this was some insane person trying to tempt her into danger by putting out research, like cheese intended to attract a mouse, so he could snap some sort of trap down on her? *Even insane people deserve a little consideration,* she thought with bleak humor.

Besides, what she could make out on the table was intriguing.

She stepped in and shut the door behind her.

"Thank you," he said. The shadowy form gestured toward the materials. "Look it over. Take your time. I'll wait."

Slowly she strode to the table and stared down. She touched nothing. She simply looked at the research, all laid out before her.

"As you see," said the voice, "it focuses on a mutual interest of ours: mutants. What causes them. And what can stop them. The fact is—and know that I will always be honest with you—I despise mutants. I think them destructive in every sense of the word—and an incredible danger to not only this world, but also to others. You, I believe, have a more…generous…point of view. It doesn't matter, because our goal is the same. Namely, to render them no longer a threat to anyone. Whether this extends from altruism or self-defense is really beside the point. Our motivations, however dissimilar they might be, intersect when it comes to the intended goal."

Rao was barely listening. Her eyes were widening with every moment as she realized what lay in front of her. Copious amounts of information, study, and data that built upon what she had done thus far and took it to the next level.

It was all right there. At last, there was hope…

"This is…it's unbelievable. I can scarcely…" Then she stopped, and a voice within warned her not to get too excited. There had to be a catch. There had to be…

"Strings," she said.

The man in the shadows sounded puzzled. "Pardon?"

"What are the strings? There are always strings attached. What sort of Faustian bargain are we talking about here? What is this going to cost me?"

"Cost?" He seemed offended at the notion. "No cost. Consider it a gift. A small boost the rest of the way to a goal you would have certainly reached on your own. Surely you see that you were very close, Doctor Rao. Your work was brilliant."

She looked back down at the research. She still couldn't help but be suspicious. "My work is what it is. And I appreciate the flattery. But frankly…Henry McCoy is the man you should be talking to. And that's not an easy thing for me to admit. There are aspects here I have to struggle to understand that he would just intuitively grasp since he's…"

"A mutant?"

"Smarter…is what I was going to say," she admitted wryly. "For all my expertise, he still exceeds me in this area. In fact, I wonder why you didn't go directly to him. He is higher profile than I am when it comes to this particular area of study."

"Perhaps. However, I don't believe Doctor McCoy would be objective about *my*…objective. Given his condition. He seems mostly preoccupied with fully understanding the mechanics of the mutant gene. Laudable, certainly, but that's a far cry from wanting to *do* something about it."

"And it's that 'something' that concerns me," said Rao. "Understand this: If I take advantage of this work…if I take it to its logical conclusion—no one is to be hurt."

"Are these *your* strings, then?" He didn't sound annoyed; indeed, he came across as slightly amused.

She nodded. "Whatever your feelings about mutants, I will not be a party to murder."

"Why, Doctor," he said chidingly, "I have just this day done the opposite. I have resuscitated a mutant your Earth-based science thought deceased."

"*What?*"

A slight rise and fall of his shoulders, as if this pronouncement were a casual accomplishment that he performed every day. "I understand your mistrust. In point of fact, I respect it. But there are millions of lives at stake and my only interest is in saving them. I don't believe you can turn your back on that opportunity."

She knew that he was right. She knew she couldn't, in fact, turn away from it. But that didn't mean she had to go into it blind, either. Boldly she came around the table and stepped right up to him. "Come into the light," she said. "I'm tired of this cloak-and-dagger nonsense."

"As you wish," he said, and did so.

She gasped as the light fell upon him. It took her long seconds to fully process who and what she was looking at.

Finally she found words:

"Is this where you say, 'Take me to your leaders?'"

"I've already been to your leaders," he said, and produced a final file that he seemed to have plucked out of nowhere. "And they gave me this."

She tentatively took the folder from him and squinted in the dimness at the name on the upper tab.

"Tildie Soames? Who's Tildie Soames?"

She flipped open the file and started reading. With each sentence she became more horrified, more distressed. The police reports, the psychiatric profiles, and the pictures, oh dear lord, the pictures filled with what was essentially a crime scene, blood and gore spattered everywhere. What must those people have felt when they died? What must they have thought? They couldn't have had the slightest comprehension of what was happening to them, and the girl, God in heaven, the girl. It was astounding that she was something other than a complete basket case, curled up in the corner of a room having gone totally fetal.

"Right now, as we speak," said this strange being who had just dropped into her life, "little Tildie is in a small, dark room. Isolated, talking to no one, fearing everything including, most particularly, herself. She's the poster girl for post-traumatic stress disorder. She has no human contact because no human will get near her, for fear of ending up the way her father and mother did. That's no way for anyone to live, much less a child. And as we both know, Doctor Rao," and he showed what passed for teeth in his massive mouth, "we must think of the children."

I was a child.

At the time I deluded myself into thinking I was an adult. Kitty Pryde, the adult. It wasn't all that tough to feel that way when I was with kids back in "normal" school. They were so freaking immature. Like that day when all the kids got together and everywhere I turned, they said, "Hello, Kitty" in these really annoying nasal voices. And all of them—girls, boys, jocks, cheerleaders, nerds, everybody—were wearing "Hello Kitty" shirts with that stupid-ass cat emblazoned on it in pink and white. And I opened my locker and—how they cracked it, I don't know—about a hundred Hello Kitty dolls fell out. And I felt so embarrassed and so frustrated and so stupid. I hated my name, I hated my stupid hair, I hated everything about everyone and everybody.

And then I left.

And I came here.

And since then, I've changed so much.

But the place hasn't. Here, nothing has changed.

As the cab pulls away, I stand in front of the building that was my home for so long. It was more than just a school. It was my haven, my salvation.

It looks just the same.

Honestly, I'm not sure I understand how it's possible. This place has been destroyed more times than the post-season hopes of Chicago Cubs fans, yet here it is, just as I remember it from the very first time I arrived. Not a brick out of place, not a dent in the roof, not a single pane of glass shattered.

Of course, the Professor would have it rebuilt this way. Give everyone a sense of stability and continuity.

Nothing has changed.

I'm standing about ten feet away from the place where

I saw Professor Xavier for what was going to be—to the best of my knowledge—the last time. I looked all fancy in my yellow suit with my stupid hair finally, *finally* smoothed out, the hated curls long gone. Professor X, in his wheelchair, looking at me with a combination of pride and wistfulness. In my mind's eye, I can see him telling me he can send my furniture to wherever I wind up, or back home to Deerfield. There I stand, my fingers interlaced, like a grown daughter heading out into the world, saying, "No. Keep it here. I intend to visit you guys every chance I get."

Liar. I'm lying so much you'd think the pants I have on now would catch fire retroactively.

The air is nippy. I'm wearing a blue flannel jacket this time. Just in case the X-Men get kidnapped again, I want to be dressed warmer than I was the first time. I have a suitcase in either hand. I've tried to prepare for any eventuality, but realistically that's not going to happen. We've seen it all: space, other dimensions, jungles, mountains, deserts. How do you pack for all that?

I phase through the wall next to the door just because I can. To my right I look at the inside of the foyer and I see my younger self, pointing an angry finger and shouting, "Professor X is a jerk!" I remember it as vividly as if it happened yesterday: Professor Xavier, deciding that my continuing to operate beside the X-Men was too dangerous, demoted me to an incoming class of students called the "New Mutants." Mutant I was, yes, but not new, and oh man, I was pissed off. I fought the decision tooth and nail and finally, after I took down a couple of bad guys single-handedly, he put me back where I belonged.

Back where I belonged.

Now where do I belong?

Perhaps I'm kidding myself. Maybe I haven't changed at all.

Because when I walk in here, all that happens is that the insecurities and uncertainties I felt when I was younger flood all over me. Despite all my experiences, despite everything I endured and went through, now that I've returned...

I'm a kid again, out of my depth. Completely overwhelmed by everything here. And it isn't any of our old enemies, the Sidri or Sentinels or the Brood, that surround me. It's the smaller pieces.

Shards. Of me.

There's the stairway I dangled the mistletoe from so I could kiss Peter Rasputin on Christmas. "Merry Christmas, sexy," purred the little kitten in his ear, and oh boy, was he shocked. I must have made the poor guy feel so uncomfortable, this pipsqueak jailbait girl coming on to him. It must have creeped him out something fierce.

I didn't care. Truthfully, I'm not even sure it occurred to me. All I cared about was him and how I felt about him and...

...and God, I miss him.

Him and Jean. She was the first X-Man to save my hash. Others did over the years, but, like they say, you never forget your first. Especially when it's today.

When it's the fifth anniversary of her death.

I put down my suitcase and compose myself. Come on, Kitty. No tears. Put on your adult face.

Nobody around. I hope I'm not late for the orientation. And hey, even if I am, it's not like it's a matter of life and death.

TWO

SCOTT Summers was dying.

He knew it. He could sense it with every fiber of his being. And yet, like a man trapped in a freight train that seemed to be derailing in slow motion, he was helpless to escape it or do anything about it.

Somebody help me. I don't want to die alone.

He looked to Hank McCoy, the Beast. Covered head to toe with blue fur, the intellectual and catlike McCoy was nattily attired in a custom-made dark-green suit and bow tie. His round glasses were perched on top of his snout. He was seated in one of the three chairs on the stage, holding the five-page speech that he had finished delivering minutes before. It had been a wonderfully irreverent discussion of the science curriculum, and it had absolutely engaged and delighted the audience. "Got them all warmed up for you,"

Hank had whispered to Scott as he slid into his seat. Scott nodded and looked down apprehensively at the small stack of index cards he'd scribbled his notes onto. He'd thought that speaking more or less off the cuff might put the audience at ease...

The audience. Scott looked out at them, staring up at him, waiting for him to say something, anything that would interest them. A sea of young faces, eager to learn what they could expect from their time at the school. The room was extremely large, with row upon row of seats set up for them. On the wall behind the speakers on the raised podium was a huge letter "X."

Emma Frost, who had introduced Scott, was now seated in the chair Scott had vacated. She was clothed in her customarily provocative style, revealing considerable midriff and cleavage. Even her lipstick was white to match her clothing. She'd had no trouble holding the students' attention...particularly the boys'. And then she'd turned the mike over to Scott and everything had gone to hell.

"I'm not quite as organized as Hank is," he'd begun. "I thought I would speak more...X-temporaneously."

He waited for the laughter. There was, instead, deathly silence, broken only by a forced chuckle here and there.

Are you done yet? Emma's voice sounded in his head.

Shut up.

Technically I'm not talking.

Shut up anyway.

All right, then.

He then proceeded to squander whatever good will Emma and Hank had built up for him with the students.

"First of all, I want you to know that if you have any questions, you can always come to me. There will be many confusing things that you will find…uhm… confusing." He winced. At least his face was covered with a visor, specially created for him with a shield made of ruby-quartz crystal that contained the powerful beams in his eyes. "All of you are here," he continued, "because you have an extra power or, if you will, X-tra power. That's where the term X-Men comes from."

A hand immediately shot up.

Scott was surprised. He hadn't expected a question that quickly. "Yes, uhm…" He racked his brains, trying to remember. "Uhm…Julian?"

"Kevin," the youngster corrected him.

"Right, Kevin. What's your question?"

"I thought it was after Professor Xavier. You know: X-avier?"

"Actually, it's pronounced Zavier. Like with a Z."

"You sure?"

"Yes, absolutely. Now, as I—"

Another hand shot up. "Yes, uh…Austin."

"Dallas."

"Yes, right, Dallas…"

"Is it pronounced Mag-nee-toe or Mag-net-oh?"

"The first one."

Five more hands shot up.

Emma Frost rose slightly from her chair and said coolly, "Let's save questions for the end of the talk."

All the hands promptly went down.

Scott went on to discuss the proud history of the school…the hopes of Professor Xavier…the sorts of challenges they could be expected to face…the social responsibility of mutantkind…

And delivered all of it in an uncomfortable monotone that suggested he would rather be anywhere else doing anything else right now.

The words continued to emerge from his mouth, but he could see the interest of the students flagging with every passing syllable. He wasn't engaging them. He was coming across like a big stiff in a red-tinted visor.

Finally, unable to endure it any longer, he said, "So, uh…if there are any questions now…?"

None were forthcoming. He glanced sidelong at Emma. Her face was an utter deadpan. He realized he couldn't be sure whether the kids simply didn't want to prolong the agony, or if Emma was beaming mental commands into their heads along the lines of, *If a single one of you asks one bloody question, you will not only regret you were born, you'll* forget *you were born.*

"Well, okay then. Thank you for listening," said Scott. There was a determined attempt at applause as Scott took his seat on the far right. Hank looked at him, face inscrutable. In a low voice, Scott leaned toward him and, indicating his index cards, said, "I had a whole section on civic pride. But I thought it'd be better to wrap it up."

"Good call," said Hank.

Emma had once again taken the podium. "Well," she said, looking with mild irritation toward the empty seat awaiting an occupant who had not yet arrived, "it would seem the proceedings will be ending a bit earlier than—"

Suddenly there was a collective gasp as a young woman's head emerged through the wall.

It was understandable. Most of the students had come from lives where they had been compelled to hide what they were. Letting on, even for an instant, that they were gifted with the mutant gene that made them Homo superior would be enough to target them for unending harassment. So suppressing any use of their powers had become second nature to many of them. As a result, they were not prepared for such casual demonstration of mutant abilities.

"Hi," said the young woman. Her face had a distinct deer-in-the-headlights look to it as she eased the rest of her body into the room. "It's possible that I'm late."

"Quite so," said Emma Frost, looking haughtily at her while gesturing toward the empty chair. Then Emma turned back to the audience. "This, children, is Kitty Pryde, who apparently feels the need to make a grand entrance."

Kitty didn't sit immediately. She was half a head shorter than Emma, but she squared her shoulders and made herself seem bigger, like a cat feeling threatened. "I'm sorry," she said, not sounding at all sorry. Her gaze flickered up and down Emma's revealing outfit. "I was busy remembering to put on all my clothes."

There were loud hoots of laughter from the students, and this time even an annoyed stare from Emma's icy blue eyes wasn't quite able to contain it.

"So gushingly glad you could join us," Emma said, and then turned back to the audience to make sure the last of the snickering was dying down. "Miss Pryde will be teaching advanced computational theory, as well as acting as a student advisor and liaison to the administrative staff."

Scott leaned over and whispered to Kitty as she took her seat, "It's great to see you."

"Sorry about the timing," she whispered back. "Did I miss the Sorting Hat?"

"Just my remarks, and Scott's scintillating introduction speech," said Hank.

Scott decided to take the comment in stride. "Even I was bored."

Emma said to the students, "Since Professor Xavier is away on sabbatical, Mr. Summers and myself will be acting heads of school. Doctor McCoy and Miss Pryde will round out the senior staff along with Logan, who is…elsewhere."

Kitty leaned toward Hank again. "What does she mean 'elsewhere'?" she whispered.

"It means we've narrowed it down to 'else.'"

They then realized that Emma had stopped speaking. Instead, she had turned around at the podium and was staring right at them. "Are we done?" she asked. "Or Miss Pryde, if you're interested in directing any remarks to the students…?"

"No, thanks, I'm good," said Kitty.

Emma nodded, then continued her remarks to the class. "Now, this is a place of learning. Not just about your mutant gifts, but about the world. Respect for your teachers, mutant and human alike, will be expected of all of you. Control of your powers. The safety of those around you, is of paramount importance. Violence of *any* kind will not be tolerated."

THREE

———————— ✦ ————————

"BRING it on. Who wants a piece?"

The bar was prime fight territory. It was small and squalid and filled with large men who had been drinking considerably and both smelled and looked like it. Country music filtered scratchily through the speakers, and no one ever really walked on the floor, which hadn't been scrubbed in possibly forever, because the inch or so of caked dirt prevented their shoes from actually touching the ground. Rumor had it that a guy from the Board of Health had been by recently to check the place, but supposedly he had simply stroked out upon seeing it and never had the opportunity to file his report.

The challenger at that particular moment was at least a head shorter than even the shortest of the behemoths chugging back beer. His black hair seemed to have a life of its own, as did his sideburns. His growling words betrayed hints of a Canadian accent.

"Logan, knock it off," said the bartender, a normally cheerful man named Clancy. "Come on…"

"*You* come on," Logan retorted. "I heard him," and he pointed at one of the largest men, a guy with a shaved and tattooed head, leaning against the pool table with a half-filled mug. "I heard what he said."

"Logan—"

"I believe I heard him say," Logan over-enunciated each word, "muttering under his breath—and these ears catch everything, trust me—that he'd never seen a sawed-off runt drink so much. Am I right?"

The bruiser cleared his throat and said, a little nervously, "Yeah, I did say that—"

"And that's gonna cost y—"

"But," he added quickly, "I was talking about him."

He pointed, and Logan's gaze flickered to a darkened corner of the bar. A little person, less than four feet tall, was sitting there with three empty mugs around him. He looked up with bleary eyes and, fixing them on the bruiser, said angrily, "My girlfriend dumped me. You got a problem with that, jerk?"

"No, no, we're cool," said the bruiser hurriedly. "Just me muttering. Didn't mean to broadcast it. Sorry, pal. How about I buy you a pint?"

The little person considered it, then said, "Long as

you don't make jokes about half-pints."

At which point the bruiser, the little person, and several others in the bar laughed aloud, all of which seemed to defuse matters until Logan stepped to within an inch of the bruiser's face and growled, "And you think that settles things?"

The bruiser gulped slightly. Everyone stood utterly paralyzed. Working to keep his voice as flat and neutral as possible, he said, "If you want, I'll buy you one, too."

Logan's nostrils flared like an animal's. "I smell fear coming off you. In waves. You that scared of me, bub? How about your friends? They scared, too? Is that what it's gonna take? Telling you what a bunch of total wimps you are, so that you'll stand up for yourself?"

The bruiser spoke barely above a whisper. "Seriously…the offer of a drink's still open…"

"No, it's not." Clancy's voice cracked sharply across the bar that was otherwise silent save for Logan's barely controlled fury. "He's cut off. You're cut off, Logan."

Slowly Logan's furious gaze turned toward Clancy. Then he walked toward the bartender, one slow step at a time, like a gunslinger, until he was right in front of the bar. "What the hell are you talking about?"

"Which word was unclear? 'Cut' or 'off'?"

"You can't cut me off, Clancy." There was no pleading in his voice. Logan was incapable of pleading. Instead it was a flat statement.

"I sure can. You want to keep having liquor served to you? Go to another bar."

"I can't do that."

"Why the hell not? There's plenty of other bars around."

Logan paused, his jaw twitching, and then he admitted in a low voice, "They *all* cut me off."

Clancy didn't understand. "What? You mean today?"

"Yeah."

Clancy took in what Logan was saying, and then called over to the bruiser that Logan had just threatened. "Jerry. Take over the bar for a minute, will ya?"

"Yeah, sure."

Clancy came around the bar as Jerry slipped in behind. He gestured for Logan to follow him, and Logan did so.

Clancy brought him around back to a storage area and turned to face him. "You telling me you've been drinking all day?"

"Yeah."

"How the hell are you even standing up? I mean, I figured you were drunk, trying to pick a fight—"

"I ain't drunk."

"That's ridiculous. You'd have to be—"

"Wanna hook me up to a breathalyzer? I'm stone-cold sober, Clancy."

Clancy looked him in the eyes. He stared for quite some time, then said, "Holy God, you are. How is that possible? Back in the bar, you were slurring your words, you were kind of wobbling…"

"Wishful thinking. My…metabolism…it fights me when it comes to getting hammered." It seemed a less complicated explanation than a mutant healing power that repaired any damage to his system so quickly that it was practically impossible for him to get drunk. He saw the way Clancy was looking at him. "You got something to say? Spit it out."

Clearing his throat, Clancy said, "Look…Logan…I've known you for a while. And I always known you're not, y'know…"

"I'm not what?"

"You're different. Okay? I dunno what your deal is, and you know what? I don't care. It's none o' my beeswax. You pay as you go, never run up a tab, which is more than I can say for some of these characters, including Jerry who's probably single-handedly gone through a quarter of my stock by now. You usually keep to yourself, and you're decent company when you're in a talkative mood. Whatever else you are, whatever else you do…*zei gezunt*, you get what I'm saying?"

"Yeah. Yeah, I get it."

"But now you're picking fights with guys? Why the hell are you doing that?"

"That's not the question," Logan said irritably. "The question is, why won't they fight? Them and the guys in other bars. I used to get into some pretty good scraps in bars. Now I insult them to their faces and they won't even defend themselves."

It was all Clancy could do not to laugh. "Of course not! Word's gotten around about you, Logan. Hell, a couple of places I know keep a picture of you behind the bar just to warn people off. Word's out that you don't mess with the short Canadian guy with the mutton chops. No offense."

Logan considered it. "Nah. That's a fair description." He looked almost forlorn. "Nobody?"

"Nobody," he said firmly. "I mean, jeez, man, you've sent guys to the emergency room and you walk away without a mark on you. Guys have pride, sure, but they're not suicidal. They figure you can call them all the names you want, but at least they'll come out of the evening in one piece, and their egos don't wind up needing a full-body cast and a hundred stitches if they get banged around. So you can go around saying what you want to pretty much anyone you want, but nobody's gonna take a swing at you because Thanksgiving's not that far off, and they don't feel like having their turkey fed to them through a tube. You get it now?"

"Yeah, I get it, okay? This has been real great, Clancy." There was a door with an exit sign on the other side of the room. "I'll just be on my way, okay?"

He headed toward the door, but stopped when Clancy said, "It's a woman, ain't it?"

He didn't look back at Clancy, keeping his face away from him. "What makes you say that?"

"Because it's always a woman. Always. What'd she do to you? Cheat on you? Dump you?"

"She died," Logan said quietly. "Five years ago. Today."

"Man, I'm sorry to hear that. What happened, if you don't mind my asking."

"Rather not say. Trust me, ya wouldn't believe me anyway. See ya later, Clancy."

"Yeah. Yeah, okay. And Logan…good luck getting drunk or picking a fight."

"Don't worry 'bout that," said Logan. "I'm a pretty resourceful guy. I'm sure I'll find a way to pull off one or the other."

And with that, he walked out and let the door slam shut behind him.

FOUR

EMMA Frost had warned that violence at the school would not be tolerated in any form. That caution was still ringing in the air when the Sentinel attacked.

There had been no warning whatsoever. One moment Emma had been finishing her speech, and the next the entire ceiling of the room was being torn away. The sun's rays filtered through in a haze of red, but no one paid any attention because they were busy dodging the debris that was tumbling from the ceiling.

Many of them had, at some point or other, seen the mutant-hunting Sentinels on television. But that hadn't really conveyed just how big the damned things truly were. This particular Sentinel was gargantuan, and seemed even bigger to the terrified students. The blue-and-purple robot was twenty feet tall, yet some would later swear that it was bigger than the Washington Monument.

And there was another one behind the first one, looking down with its expressionless face and perpetually glowing yellow eyes.

A handful of the students actually responded in a manner that was appropriate to beings of their nature and power. One young boy left the ground, flying as quickly as he could between the bits of falling debris. Another student, an Asian girl with a look that was both frightened and determined, created a force field that conformed to the shape of her body, as if it were some manner of energized armor.

The vast majority, however, scrambled to get out of the way of the oncoming threat. "Mutants targeted," rumbled the nearer Sentinel, and several of the students were knocked off their feet and nearly trampled in the rush to get away. The Sentinels, they knew, had been created specifically to seek and destroy mutants.

Scott Summers was on his feet. Memories of his boring speech were immediately banished from the minds of the students as he snapped open his visor and they beheld Cyclops in action. A red beam of energy lashed out, blasting into the nearest of the Sentinels, staggering the gigantic robot but not stopping him. Hank McCoy was yanking clear his necktie, all semblance of the erudite and urbane individual from minutes earlier gone and replaced by a snarling creature that truly fit the name "Beast."

Kitty Pryde backed up, phasing right through her chair. Her power gave her limited offensive capabilities, but she was studying the oncoming robot carefully, looking for some sort of weakness, some opportunity she could seize to fight back against the unwanted intruder.

And as people screamed and energy blasts ripped through the air and the Beast unleashed a defiant roar, and as the students were nearly killing each other just to get clear of the terrifying, towering robot that was coming right at them...

...Emma calmly touched a device sitting atop her podium.

Just like that, the Sentinels faded away. The debris likewise disappeared and the ceiling fixed itself, the hole vanishing to be replaced by a flat sheet of metal.

It was difficult for the students to process the idea that they were no longer under attack. Their collective pulse was still extremely high. One of them leaned against the wall, dramatically clutching at his chest. (He would later be found to be suffering from heartburn.)

Finally, all eyes turned to Emma, who was standing precisely where she had been, utterly indifferent to the pandemonium she'd caused.

"So. What have we learned?" she said, as casually

as one might ask a child coming home from kinder-garten. "Anyone? Anyone?" No one replied. Small wonder. The students were busy composing them-selves, and Cyclops, Beast, and Kitty were just glaring at her, irritated about becoming pawns in Emma's little battle of wits.

"We have learned," she went on, "that they will always hate us. We will never live in a world of peace. Which is why control and non-violence are essential. We must prove ourselves a peaceful people. We must give the ordinary humans respect, compliance, and understanding. And we must never mistake that for trust. All right, you all have your room assignments. Classes start tomorrow. Dismissed."

She watched the shaken students file out. Some of them were still trembling, and there were nervous mutterings of, "Is that gonna happen all the time around here?"

Kitty approached Emma and snapped at her, "I should have known. Holding the orientation in the Danger Room…I should have known you'd pull some sort of holographic stunt just to scare the crap out of them."

"Yes. You should have," said Emma, not the least bit put out by Kitty's clear annoyance. "Perhaps you weren't sufficiently prepared the first time you attended this school. You may want to take a refresher course or two. You might find some of my lectures useful."

"Yeah? What are you teaching? Defense against the Dark Arts?"

"Next semester, perhaps."

Emma descended from the podium, one elegant stride at a time. Hank walked to the edge, no less annoyed than Kitty. His shirt was half open and his glasses were in his hand. "Are you aware what could have happened here, Emma?"

"It was a calculated risk."

"Those kids," and he pointed a clawed finger, "were in a panic. One or more of them could have been badly injured in the stampede. Did you factor that into your calculations?"

"Yes, I did. Just as I factored in that everybody is the hero in their own narrative." One delicate eyebrow arched on her chiseled face. "Everyone imagines that, when faced with danger, they're going to save the day. It leads to overconfidence, which in turn leads to death. These children are just beginning to learn the harsh realities of being a mutant in a world in which people would just as soon kill them as look at them. They need a baseline from which to start, an honest assessment of where they are now, so they can understand just how far they need to go. Every student here who shrieked or ran or soiled her or himself, the first time they faced what they believed to be true danger, is going to be shamed by that reaction. They have been forced to face themselves and they'll know they were found wanting. It will give them something to aspire to, someplace to build from, so that when the real thing comes for them—as it inevitably will—they'll be ready. Or at least as ready as we can make them. Oh, and by the way, Doctor McCoy..." She smiled thinly. "Love the glasses. Marvelous disguise. When you wear them, I can't even tell it's you."

Then she looked to Scott. A moment frozen in time. Even Kitty and Hank turned to Scott to see whether he had something to say.

He said nothing. He simply stood there and stared at her, his face devoid of any expression.

That silent moment seemed to extend indefinitely. Then, without another word, Emma turned and walked away, her hips swishing back and forth.

"Nice going, Scott," said Kitty. "You sure told her."

"We'll discuss it," said Scott. "Just not here and not now."

"When, then?"

"When I calm down."

He strode away, leaving Kitty and Hank looking at each other.

"He was angry?" she said.

"Actually, he was," said Hank. "You could see the edge of his mouth twitching slightly. That's how you know."

* * * *

THEIR paths didn't cross again for the rest of the day, and it wasn't until they were in the suite they shared that Scott finally had the opportunity to talk to Emma face-to-face.

The suite had two desks, one for each of them, which faced each other. There was also a sitting area where they would meet with students who needed personal time with either of them. Historically, and interestingly—although perhaps not that surprisingly—the male students gravitated to Emma while the females would gaze longingly at Scott. Scott had once asked her if she ever quietly eavesdropped on the boys' thoughts. She'd laughed and said, "Trust me, I could be bereft of telepathic powers—not to mention deaf, dumb, and blind—and I'd still know what they're thinking."

Now they stood opposite each other, leaning against their respective desks. Scott's arms were folded across his chest, while Emma was leaning back, her arms at her sides, hands flat on the desktop and—Scott couldn't help but notice—her hips thrust slightly forward. *She's trying to distract you,* he thought. *Don't let her do it. Don't let her do it.*

"You should have told me you were going to do that," he said, all business.

"You would have said no."

"Among other things."

"I feel it's always better to ask forgiveness than permission."

She said it in a slightly teasing voice, but Scott wasn't going for it. He kept his expression stern. "Everything both Kitty and Hank said was right."

"As was everything I said. Or don't I get points for that?"

"Being right wouldn't have mattered if there'd been a fatality. How are we preparing children for the future if they have no future because the lessons killed them? We both know that once that chaos was unleashed, once they started running, anything could have happened. Someone could have died..."

"Then they had better do it and decrease the surplus population."

It took him a moment, but then he got it. "You're Scrooge now, is that it? Is that how you want people to think of you? Heartless and uncaring?"

"Scott, in all the years you've known me, have I ever given a damn about what people think of me?"

It was a fair question.

"No," he admitted. "On the other hand, I don't think you're heartless and uncaring, which leads me to wonder why you'd want anyone to think you are?"

"I would also point out," she said, "that the line about the surplus population was said by the Ghost of Christmas Present, who was mocking Scrooge's opinions. And Christmas Present loved mankind beyond all things."

"So you're saying you did it because you love our students so much."

"Sometimes you have to be cruel to be kind," she said with a shrug of her shapely shoulders.

He still wasn't swayed. "What you did wasn't right, and the proof that even *you* knew that is that you didn't ask me."

She let out an annoyed sigh. Her tone went from wheedling to resigned and business-like. "During orientation, I scanned the students. Nearly ten percent of them were more than a little excited at the prospect of a fight. I thought we should know—"

"Which ones were," he completed the thought. "To know who might have the most capability for joining a fighting force...and who might be the most reckless and possibly get themselves killed in a real fight. It's a valid point and one I'd *almost* buy—except you were the one who decided we should have the orientation in the Danger Room. Which makes it come across to me as if it were more premeditated than something you just decided to do on the spur of the moment."

"Why are we wasting time with verbal fencing, Scott? It was a valid exercise in student assessment, and whether it was planned ahead, spur of the moment, or a little bit of both, really doesn't matter. Although for the record, where else would we have orientation except in the Danger Room? It's the largest room in the mansion, unless you wanted to have it down in the hangar bay...in which case, most of the students would have been busy looking at the Blackbird."

The Blackbird was the X-Men's transport of choice, a sleek aircraft that had begun its life as a simple spy plane. Since then the ship had acquired concussive missiles and other weaponry.

"I don't know about that. With you on the podium, who could possibly be distracted by anything else?"

"Good heavens, Scott." She stood upright and began to sashay over toward him in a manner that was determinedly coquettish. "Is that a *compliment*? A few more like that and you might actually turn my head."

"There's always that possibility." He thought a moment, and then said, "The students...which ones were—?"

"I'm not Professor Xavier, Scott, despite our many physical similarities," she said wryly. "As much as it pains me to admit it, as a telepath I'm not remotely on his level. He can wield his mind like a surgeon does a scalpel. I'm more of a sledgehammer. I can't pinpoint with that facility, especially when it comes to new minds that I'm encountering for the first time. But if you'd like, I'll go through the roster and try to narrow it down..."

She was close enough then to rest her hand on his chest. She gazed into the red slit in his visor that kept him blocked off from the rest of the world. "...tomorrow."

"Not tonight."

"No," and her gaze flickered toward the door at the

far end of the suite: the door that led to their bedroom. "I have other plans for tonight."

"And they include me."

"Well, I *could* start without you, but I'd much rather you joined me."

She's trying to distract you again. Don't let her do it. Don't let her do it.

He let her do it.

And later, when the clothes came off and their bodies came together, they were able to escape—just for a moment—from the truth that neither of them wanted to admit or even think about:

Some of those kids *were* going to die. What had happened that day in the Danger Room was simply a dress rehearsal for the actual, brutal demise that awaited some of them. There was no way of knowing which ones it would be, but there would be some. There might be many. It could be all of them.

And every single person who died would do so for one reason and one reason only. Because the two people in the bed, who were trying desperately to lose themselves in each other, hadn't managed to get the job done, had failed to prepare the students for what they were going to face. The deaths of those young people, whether it came in one year or five or fifty, would result because Scott and Emma and the other teachers hadn't been good enough.

This awareness of a future speeding toward them

like a freight train was something they carried with them every hour of every day. But if they could escape the nightmares that dogged their heels for even a moment, that would make this a good night. A very good night.

FIVE

LITTLE Tildie Soames is having a terrible night.

Her parents have been arguing loudly for the past half hour, very loudly, saying all those words that Tildie knew she wasn't supposed to say. Things were broken, and her mother just stormed upstairs declaring she was going to bed because she had a migraine. And that loud argument has sunk into Tildie's dreaming mind, raising Cain and far worse things than that.

Her dreams are haunting her, terrible creatures moving through them, huge awful things with knives for teeth and saws for fingers and six eyes, or at least she thinks they're eyes, oozing something that looks like a combination of blood and pus. They are banging against the door of her closet, and even though they have not yet emerged she knows exactly what they look like because they are her nightmares, her own night terrors made manifest.

In her dreamlike state, walking that borderline where the separation of reality from fantasy is at its thinnest, she clambers out of bed. Her bare feet touch the hardwood floor and it's cold, so cold, and she pads across it and out into the hallway toward the safety of the only place she can think of where monsters would not dare to follow.

Her parents' bedroom door is partly open, which means she can go in. She knows better than to try to do so when it's closed because the last time she did that her parents were all tumbling in the sheets and breathing hard, and they yelled at her and she didn't like it at all.

Her mother is lying there, and Tildie clambers into bed with her. Mother's wearing a flannel nightgown. Tildie puts her body up against her, taking solace in the feel of the flannel and the warmth of her mother, the security of her steady breathing, her bosom raising up and down rhythmically.

The monster cannot attack her here.

And she hears the closet door burst open from down the hallway.

Her spine stiffens; her sphincter tightens. She stops breathing.

The monster could not possibly know where I am.

It's approaching, its claws clicking on the hallway floor.

The monster would not dare come in here.

The bedroom door bangs open, and Mommy, startled by the noise, sits up, looking confused, caught in that same place of half-awake/half-asleep that has Tildie in its clutches. "What the—?" The words sound thick like syrup, and suddenly Mommy screams and clutches Tildie to herself protectively, and she screams again and the monster charges forward, grabbing at Tildie, yanking her out of her mother's grasp. It pulls Tildie into it, and it's only at that moment Tildie realizes the monster is a she, a female, a mother itself, and it wants Tildie for its very own. It shoves Tildie into its body and Tildie is floating in the air, a part of it now, trapped, and her mother screams inarticulately, lunging for it. Mommy is screaming and Tildie is sharing the monster's thoughts, and the monster is thinking, "Her screams are yummy." And the monster reaches out and grabs her mother by either arm and starts to pull, and suddenly Tildie is back in the schoolyard, watching that icky Hunter Jenkins plucking the wings off a writhing fly, and Tildie's mother has time for just one shriek before her body is ripped in half, right down the middle. Blood is everywhere, on the bed, on the wall, on the tongue of the monster that savors it, on everything except Tildie herself who continues to float helplessly, and Tildie is screaming but her screams are muffled by the monster.

Her father is at the door, fully dressed in his day clothes, shouting things like "What the hell is going on up here? Did you drag Tildie into this?" She tries to yell, tries to tell her father to run, but he stands there paralyzed, his eyes wide with horror, and the monster goes for him, grabs him, guts him, the blades going into him so easily, like knives slicing into butter, and her daddy stares down at what's seeping from his gut, trying desperately to shove pink tubes and other stuff back into where it's supposed to go. He sags to his knees and there's gurgling sounds coming from his mouth, which the monster doesn't seem to like all that much, so the monster picks him up and slams him against the wall to stop him from gurgling.

Then come the red lights that flood the room, the red lights that she doesn't understand, and there are two more men at the door, policemen. Policemen are her friends. She knows this because one of them came to school a few months ago and told them so. He'd had a bright, shiny badge and a dog, and a gun in his holster that he wouldn't remove so the boys could see it, no matter how much they begged him to.

There is no dog now and she can see the guns clearly, both pointed at her, and the monster lashes out with its free hand (its other hand is still buried in Daddy's chest) and drives its fist straight through the chest of the nearest policeman. It lifts him clear off his feet, pinning him against the wall like a butterfly, and the second policeman's hands are trembling as he fires his gun, and the bullet is coming right at her and she's going to die she's going to—

"Veeda!" she cried.

Tildie jerked awake, her short brown hair hanging in front of her eyes, covering the narrow scar on her forehead. Her nightgown was plastered on her sweating body. She was shaking uncontrollably, the images she'd just seen glued to the insides of her eyeballs. The small bedroom that had become the be-all and end-all of her world was dark, and in the darkness she was sure, she was absolutely positive, that the monsters were lurking again. They had enfolded her into themselves, or itself, or however many selves they were, and had—as a consequence—taken up permanent residence within her, waiting for their moment to escape and wreak more havoc. "Veeda!" she screamed again, and then the room was suddenly filled with light.

It was not a particularly large room. The walls were pink, and there was a single dresser that was nevertheless large enough to contain all her clothes, save for the blood-soaked nightgown she hadn't seen since That Night (It had been analyzed thread by thread and was now in a plastic bag safely tucked away in a locker she would never see.) And there was that large mirror on the other side of the room. She'd never seen a mirror quite so large and didn't understand the need for it, but otherwise she didn't give it any thought.

Veeda stood framed in the doorway. Veeda was the only person she ever saw these days. Veeda, with her brown skin and that pretty red dot on her forehead, was also the only person she cared about, because Veeda cared about her. Veeda had, through no means Tildie understood, taken her away from the dark cell and the scary people who had put her there and who had treated her like *she* was the nightmare that everyone should be afraid of.

"Tildie, sweetie, I'm right here." Her voice had that strange accent, but it didn't matter. Nothing mattered except that Veeda was where she needed her to be.

"It came back!" Tildie cried out. "I saw it! I felt it! I—"

Veeda sat on the edge of the bed and took the child into her arms. "It was just a dream, Tildie," she said soothingly.

Tildie clutched at the fabric of Veeda's white lab coat. It was just like the coat Tildie's pediatrician had worn, back when Tildie had had a pediatrician and a mother to take her to him. Veeda wore it for the same reason: She was a doctor. That was all Tildie had needed to hear when they'd first met. Everyone knew doctors made you better, and if Veeda could make her better, that was all Tildie wanted.

"I don't have 'just dreams,'" Tildie whispered, her voice as ominous as any child's could be.

"Yes. You do. Now you do, just like anybody else."

"I don't want it to come back." She glanced around nervously, as if worried "it" might hear her.

"It never will, Tildie," Veeda assured her. "It never will."

DOCTOR Kavita Rao remained with Tildie, cradling Tildie's head on her shoulder until the child drifted back into what Rao could only pray would be a dreamless sleep. Then she eased the girl back down onto the pillow. She didn't turn the lights out immediately, though. Instead she remained there, watching the child, making sure there was no repetition of the episode before finally shutting off the lights and closing the door.

She then came around to the observation room. Her "associate" was standing there waiting for her, staring through the one-way mirror that allowed the girl to be observed without knowing it was happening.

"When was the last time you went home and got a good night's sleep?" he rumbled. In some ways he was no less disconcerting than he had been the night he had first come to her.

"A lifetime ago," she said, rubbing the fatigue from her eyes. She'd been monitoring all of Tildie's vitals during the girl's slumber and, to her shame, had drifted off, awakened by Tildie's scream. Fortunately enough they didn't have to do anything as intrusive as taping wires to the child to keep track of what was going on in her mind and body. The monitoring systems had been built into the bed.

He glanced toward the slumbering girl. "How bad was it?"

"Her REM sleep, you mean? As bad as it gets. Her brain activity was off the charts."

"So there is every reason to believe it was identical to the dreams that caused the manifestations resulting in the termination of her parents' lives."

She stared at him. "I wouldn't have put it quite that clinically, but yes. Based on what she told me—and I have no reason to think she was lying—she was experiencing the exact same dreams that killed her parents and the police officer."

Her associate sniffed disdainfully. "The parents I could understand, but there was no excuse for the policeman. He was armed and a warrior. He had no business being killed by a girl's dream manifestations."

"I'm sorry not everyone can be on a par with you," she said.

"It is not your fault, and thus you have no reason to apologize."

There seemed no point in explaining concepts such as sarcasm to him. "Thank you."

"You're welcome. So," he said briskly, "if her nightmares were going to manifest in any way, they would have done so during this incident."

"Yes, absolutely." She checked over the instruments. "But there was nothing. No psychokinetic manifestations at all. Her tank, so to speak, is empty. By every possible scientific measure, she's free of it." She took a moment to process the fact, closing her eyes, breathing deeply, letting it out. Tears stung at the corners of her eyes, an uncharacteristically emotional response to the assessment of scientific data. "She's free of it," she said again.

"In that case, Doctor," he said, "I believe it's time you told the world, so that others know there is hope for them at last."

"Yes. Hope. That's exactly right. I'll make the arrangements." Then she paused and looked up at him tentatively. "Are you going to be there? Make your presence known? I could not have done it without you."

"Remember our agreement, Doctor. Insofar as the world knows, that is in fact exactly what you did. I will not have it any other way. And besides," and what passed for a smile played across his lips, "when you're having your press conference, I have plans to be... elsewhere."

"Do I want to know where?"

"I think it wiser that you do not."

She took him at his word.

SIX

THE gentle rays of the morning sun filtered through the bedroom window. Emma was just beginning to awaken, but she had not yet opened her eyes. It was her experience that the moment she opened her eyes was typically the point at which the day began to head downhill. So she remained where she was, her right arm draped over the bare chest of the sleeping Scott Summers.

The sheets were twisted around her. This told her that Scott had had a restless night, which never boded well. It told her that Scott had had a lot of dreams, and he wasn't someone who could typically shake them off come morning light. They usually wound up having an impact on the rest of the day, making him brood even more than usual.

Please don't let it be about her.

That was Emma's greatest fear. She knew perfectly well that yesterday had been the fifth anniversary of Jean Grey's death. Scott's great lost love, the red-haired, telepathic bint that he had been devoted to since practically the first day she'd walked into the school as a callow teenager. The woman he had loved, and married, and lost.

Scott had said nothing about it, though. Hadn't waxed nostalgic for her, hadn't stood longingly in front of her portrait that hung there in the den, a constant reminder of her absence. Emma wondered if it was possible that he'd forgotten. That would have been nice, a sign that he was finally, *finally,* moving on. Not being rooted in the past was the only way they, Emma and Scott, could have a hope of proceeding into a real future.

At least he hadn't woken up shouting Jean's name or something hopelessly melodramatic like that. Maybe he'd just had dreams of walking into a test unprepared, or standing on stage naked in the middle of a play he hadn't rehearsed for and didn't know any of the lines. Nice, mundane stuff like that, which wouldn't have any impact on his mood.

It would be really nice if this were a good day for once.

And then a rough, growling voice shattered any hope of that.

"So tell me…"

Emma immediately sat up. Scott was instantly jolted awake, the glow behind his visor snapping on like a refrigerator light. A lethal, highly concussive refrigerator light.

Wolverine was perched on the footboard of the bed, the sun coming up behind him as if it were anxious to try to get a good view of what was going on. His feet were bare, enabling him to balance. His shirt hung open, revealing his hirsute chest. Alcohol rolled off his breath in waves; he smelled like he'd consumed an entire distillery.

"...which stage of grieving is this?" said Wolverine. "Denial?"

I'm going to kill him, thought Emma.

Scott, as it happened, was way ahead of her. His visor snapped open and a blast of pure crimson force erupted from his head. It slammed into Logan before he could move...

No, Emma thought. *Nothing happens before he can move. He wanted to get hit. He wanted to fight...or maybe he just wants to be punished because he wasn't able to save* her...

...and sent Logan hurtling backwards. The glass in the window exploded outward as he soared through the air and landed heavily on the back lawn.

"Scott!" shouted Emma, but he was already gone, out the bedroom door. She heard his feet seconds later, pounding down the stairs. It was a damned good thing he was wearing pajama pants. If he'd been sleeping in the nude, the students would have gotten one hell of a show.

The students.

She closed her eyes in pain. Terrific. This was going to be a great start to the day.

Emma shifted her attention back out to the lawn, where Wolverine was bounding to his feet as Scott charged to confront him. She didn't have to listen in through their minds; their voices were carrying across the lawn.

"Strike a nerve, Summers?" said Wolverine. His claws snapped out from his fists with their customary, unique *snikt* sound. "What happened? Emma Frost do a conscience-ectomy on ya?"

"This is good," Scott retorted. "The guy who tried to steal my wife since the day he met us is gonna tell me all about what's *proper.*"

Wolverine grinned lopsidedly. "Only reason Jean and you stayed together at all is she was too strong to give in to what she really wanted...and you were too scared."

"Hey Logan," said Scott as he reached for the side of his visor, "that healing power's about to come in really handy."

Wolverine leaped straight up to avoid the blast he knew was coming at him, but Scott knew Wolverine's moves too well. He aimed his blast not at where Wolverine was, but where he knew the angry mutant was going to be. The crimson beam struck Logan broadside and sent him flying a half-mile into a thicket of large oak trees.

There was no movement for a long moment, and then leaves started flying everywhere. Wolverine was cutting his way out of the tangle of branches so he could get at Scott.

To hell with them. I hope they kill each other, Emma thought. And she was only partly joking.

HANK McCoy, whose suite of offices was directly across the hall from Scott and Emma's, ran into the bedroom to see what was going on, unceremoniously clad only in an undershirt and boxers. He stopped short, staring at the shattered window and at Emma, who wore a white negligee with nothing under it. Quickly, out of a sense of decorum, he averted his eyes as Emma said drily, "Good morning, Henry. I see everyone's getting the day off to an early start."

He crossed quickly toward the window and stared out. Scott was standing in the middle of the lawn. A flood of students were pouring out, with what looked to be Kitty Pryde leading the pack. In the distance, there appeared to be some sort of mutant leaf blower trapped in a grove of trees, doing its best to denude the upper branches of Hank's favorite oak. When Wolverine leapt out and started toward Scott, all became clear.

Except not really.

"What's this all about?" Hank asked.

"What do you think?" Emma said. She was trying to sound indifferent, but the bitterness in her voice was unmistakable. "Super-powers, a scintillating wit, and the best body money can buy...and I still rate below a corpse."

Then it became truly clear.

Hank McCoy couldn't remember the last time, if ever, that he had actually felt sorry for Emma Frost. He tried to find the words to say, but hadn't a clue what they would be.

"I don't need your pity," Emma said. "What I need right now is a shower. I suddenly feel unclean."

She walked into the bathroom, and as the door clicked shut, Hank returned his attention to the battle outside. At that moment he didn't know whether to go to the bathroom door and offer words of consolation... or go out and try to settle this stupidity down before someone got hurt...or just go nuke some popcorn, kick back and watch the show.

SCOTT'S fists were trembling with rage as he saw Wolverine heading toward him again.

The little bastard. Did he really think I'd forgotten about Jean? Did he really think she's ever far from my thoughts? That I'm not haunted by her? This isn't about me at all. This is about him trying to "prove" that he loved her more than I did. That he can't do anything but drink to kill the pain while I'm busy trying to run a school and prepare young people for their danger-filled lives. He's trying to show me up, just like he's done from day one, and even though Jean's gone five years, he's still trying to impress her, to…

There was a loud clearing of a female throat.

Scott turned and saw Kitty standing there, her arms folded across the extra-large pink hockey jersey she wore. She was scowling fiercely, disapproval on her face. Other students had followed her out, gaping at the display in front of them.

Scott felt the weight of their stares upon him. Any number of times in the past, he'd squared off with Logan about something or other…usually the same thing. But most times either they'd been alone, or else there had been other members of the team present, trying to get between them…

The team.

Those two words exploded in Scott's mind with the same intensity of light as his eye beams. They reminded him of various thoughts that had been rattling around in his head lately. An unease, a frustration that had been growing daily, a conviction that the X-Men might be going in the wrong direction. That they had the potential to accomplish so much, and none of that potential was being tapped.

The words reminded him of what he truly had in mind for the current faculty, and he felt annoyed that he had allowed himself to be so easily distracted from his true objectives. Mentally he kicked himself…

His head whipped around. Wolverine was upon him. Scott had been so lost in thought that he had lost track of Logan.

His reflexes, honed by thousands of battles, served him well. A heartbeat before Wolverine's claws reached him, he fired off another blast. Wolverine had been leaping toward him in an arc; the beam caught him at its apex, blasting the tattered remains of his shirt right off him. Wolverine spiraled through the air and hit the ground.

"We're done," said Scott crisply.

"Oh, no we ain't." Wolverine got to his feet. He was unsteady, but Scott knew that would pass. He did not, however, care.

"You want to stab me in the back? Be my guest if you're that desperate to prove you're the better man." He turned and walked away from Wolverine without giving him a second glance.

Wolverine took two quick steps after him, but Kitty Pryde interposed her body between the two men. "Don't even," she said.

Wolverine stopped in his tracks, regarding her with faint annoyance. Then he sheathed his claws and muttered, "Y'know, half-pint, you still ain't too grown-up for me to give ya a good paddling."

"Better than you have tried," she said. Then she turned and ran after Scott.

She caught up with him as the rest of the students were left milling on the front lawn. "So…I missed the memo about morning calisthenics. Maybe you should have gone for jumping jacks to start, and then worked your way up to trying to kill each other…"

"Not now, Kitty."

"Yes, now, Scott," she said in a low, frustrated voice. "How the hell are we supposed to drill any sense of community into these kids if we can't even—"

"I'm away ahead of you."

"We have to stand for something!"

"As I said, way—"

Henry wants to know if you're quite through making fools of each other while the new students look on? Emma's irritated voice sounded in Scott's head. *Or are you and Mr. Pointy planning to take this indoors so we can have some more property damage? Because if so, then by all means, go to it. With every tenth insurance claim, we get a free toaster, and I think this'll be number nine…*

He ignored her obvious frustration. He understood it. Hell, he was responsible for it. *Senior staff,* he said telepathically, *in the Danger Room in ten minutes.*

To hell with that. It was Logan's voice. Obviously Emma had instantly conveyed Scott's sentiments to the others, and Logan was making his feelings known through the shared mental link. *I don't feel like sittin' down in a room with One-eye right now. Forget it.*

Emma's voice snapped back at him. *You want to talk about forgetting things, Logan? Either you be there, or else you're going to forget everything you ever knew about yourself. I'll construct an entirely new identity for you and send you out into the world to find your new destiny.*

You can't do that. But he sounded slightly uncertain.

I guarantee you, in your next life, you will be a musical-theater god. And I'll make sure we have front-row seats for every performance.

There was a pause. Scott wouldn't have thought it was possible to growl telepathically, but apparently it was. *Fine,* Logan growled.

Good. I'll have Henry prepare the Danger Room.

Scott wasn't wild about the sound of that. He liked Emma's unpredictability. It was part of what made their relationship stimulating. This time, though, he was a little concerned with what she was going to come up with. Especially if she was putting her head together with the formidable Doctor McCoy.

* * * *

"I still can't believe I was seeing what I was seeing. And in front of the students!" said Hank McCoy as he stood knee-deep in the Pacific Ocean.

Like modern-day Gullivers in the land of the Lilliputians, Scott, Kitty, Logan, and Emma towered over an assortment of Hawaiian islands. Clouds danced around their heads as a three-dimensional relief map of Hawaii was spread out all around them. Scott imagined he could hear teeny tiny Hawaiians running, screaming in terror as the gigantic mutants sat on the various islands.

Hank continued venting his frustration over the recent display. "And if Emma's little game yesterday didn't wind them up enough, they have to see their administrative staff trying to kill each other! These kids are supposed to look up to you!"

"I hate this," said Emma.

"Well, I know you weren't responsible for their wretched behavior, Emma, but yesterday *was* your responsibility—"

"No, it's not that. How did I wind up on Oahu?" She looked down, annoyed, at the island she was sitting on. "I wouldn't be caught dead in Oahu. Honolulu is where all the tourists go because the cheap resorts are here. When I go to Hawaii, I stay in Maui. Katherine, switch with me."

"Screw you," Kitty retorted, holding firmly on to Maui. "I'm busy trying not to step on Lana'i and Kahoolawe. You'd just wipe them out with your big feet."

"My feet are not big."

Hank scowled fiercely. "Ladies, I don't do well with being ignored—"

"Kauai's nice," suggested Logan who was cooling his heels on Molokai. "That's free. You could move one over."

"Absolutely not. I had the worst dinner of my life there. I was sick for three days."

"Fine, whatever." He glanced across the ocean at Scott. "Of course *he* gets the *Big* Island. Compensating much there, Slim?"

"Look who's talking."

"*People!*" Hank raised his voice angrily. "Perhaps you think this is funny, but I—" He sighed when he saw that Kitty was raising her hand. "Yes. What?"

"It's just that…I kind of really don't know why I'm here," said Kitty. "I didn't get in anybody's face, I didn't get into a fight with anybody…"

"You were late yesterday," said Emma.

"Yeah," Kitty said, "you really gotta learn to let things go, which I know might sound like kind of a weird idea, considering this bunch nurses so many grudges it's like you all have cast-iron nipples…" Clouds started to drift into her face. She brushed them away in annoyance. "Ack! This is…is this like a theme thing, us being so big? Going with the whole 'looking up to us' bit?"

Hank was still incredibly frustrated that he wasn't managing to impress upon them how angry he was, but he was also a bit chagrined that Kitty had pointed that out. "Actually, it's my fault," he admitted. "I programmed the Danger Room to replicate Hawaii because I thought it would relax our combatants. It appears I should have been more specific about scale." He pulled out a remote control and started reconfiguring.

Kitty was able to shoo away the last bits of the cloud, but not before it managed to moisten her head. "Great. Now I have cloud hair. Remember when this place was just flame-throwers and rotating knives? I miss that."

"As I was saying," Hank said testily while he continued to work on the remote, "Scott, Logan...you two should be long past that nonsense."

"I'm not apologizing to Logan, and I wouldn't accept one in return."

"Scott," Hank said, "you're acting head of the—"

But Scott put up a hand, interrupting him. "It was inexcusable, I agree. And it's going to make what I have to say all the more absurd, but I'm going to say it anyway." He paused, and then said, "We're a team. We're a super hero team. And I think it's time we started acting like one."

"Ho, whoa, wait," said Logan. "Is this gonna be about tights?"

Despite the frustrating circumstances that had forced them into this idiotic situation, Hank couldn't help but smile a bit to himself. He had no desire to act like the hall monitor from hell and he had resented the hell out of Logan and Scott—especially Scott—for putting him into this situation. If Scott was ready to pull his cranium out of his nether regions and act like a leader instead of a brawler, then Hank was happy to listen.

SEEING that Hank looked a bit less angry than before, Scott relaxed slightly. Of everyone in the room, he and Hank went back the furthest. They were the only two people there from the original team, brought together by the dream of Charles Xavier. Because of that, Hank's support for Scott's new vision was the most important to him.

"It's about everything," said Scott. "Truth. Perception. We've saved the world—*worlds,* even—time and again. That's the truth. That's what we do." Two dolphins were copulating against his ankle. He ignored them. "But the perception is that we're freaks or worse. That we're Magnetos, just waiting to happen. We've been taking it on the chin so long, just trying to keep from being wiped out, I think we've forgotten that we have a purpose." He stood up and pointed east toward the mainland, far in the distance. "I know the rest of the world has forgotten. The point is—"

He turned back to them and was startled to find that they were all standing on a normally proportioned beach. The water gently lapped up to their toes. He could hear the dolphins in the distance making loud, high-pitched sounds. He knew why they were doing it, and realized he'd never hear dolphin noises the same way again. Hank nodded with satisfaction at the remote control.

"The point is simply this: We need to get into the world. Saving lives, helping with disaster relief. We need to present ourselves as a team like any other. Avengers, Fantastic Four—they don't get chased through the streets with torches and pitchforks…"

"Here come the tights," Wolverine said under his breath.

"Sorry, Logan," said Scott, trying to sound sympathetic and not succeeding terribly well. "Super heroes wear costumes. And quite frankly, all the black leather is making people nervous."

Kitty put up her hand again, then glanced at it self-consciously and lowered it as she said, "Okay, I officially, really, *really* don't know why I'm here. I'm not a fighter. Not like you guys."

"You've been in it plenty, kid. I'd take you at my back any day." Only Wolverine could take a compliment and make it sound like a grudging admission.

"But you're not a fighter," Scott agreed with her. "Your power isn't aggressive, it's protective. That's good to show. You're likable. Even Logan likes you. Which says something." Logan tilted his head slightly in mute agreement. "Hank's articulate as anything, but what people see is mostly…well…a Beast. Emma's a former villain, Logan's a thug—"

"Born and bred," said Logan.

"And me," Scott said, "I can lead a team, but I haven't looked anybody in the eye since I was fifteen."

"So I'm…what? A P.R. stunt?" Kitty was clearly not sure she liked the sound of that.

"Yes, our own little poster child. Isn't that sweet?" Emma said with what sounded like a purr. "The 'Nonthreatening Shadowcat' or 'Sprite' or 'Ariel'—a made-up compound noun, a brand of soda, and a cartoon mermaid—or whatever incredibly unimpressive name you're using nowadays."

"Emma, shut up," said Scott.

Emma had almost as practiced a poker face as Scott, but this time she reacted with visible surprise at the rebuke. Scott ignored her. "You all may have perfectly good reasons for not wanting to do this, but you're the team I chose. So think about it."

There was dead silence for a long moment, and then Hank finally said what absolutely none of them were thinking:

"Am I the only one who's dying to see the outfits?"

I don't know what to make of it.

I go back to my room, get showered, wash cloud out

of my hair, get dressed. I only have one actual class today and, considering I've never actually taught someone, I don't do a half-bad job of it. As I walk through the hall-ways, I hear kids muttering about the big fight they saw in the morning. "I thought they were supposed to be super heroes," one of them says, and another replies, "Super heroes always fight each other. It's how they say 'hello.'"

Super heroes. Such a stupid phrase. I'm not even sure what that means. The obvious thing is that it's someone with super-powers, but there are guys with no extraordinary powers who the public calls super heroes. What's required to be one? You take on an assumed name, wear some kind of protective armor, carry a weapon, and try to right wrongs with a sidekick following you around? By those criteria, Don Quixote was a super hero.

Stupid phrase. Probably trademarked, too. Knowing our luck, if we start getting called super heroes, whoever holds the trademark is going to come around and send us a cease-and-desist letter. Maybe charge us a hundred bucks for every use.

I go for a stroll in the latter part of the afternoon. Sun's setting earlier these days, but it won't be dark for a while. The back lawn's empty. No one's trying to beat the crap out of each other. That's a plus.

Even as I dwell on the things that Scott was talking about, I shove them aside and start to worry about some-thing else. I look to the skies and they're empty. Someone should be here who isn't, and it's starting to concern me.

"You see something, kid?" Logan's voice, practically at my elbow. How the hell does he do that? I guess I shouldn't be surprised, though. This is a guy whose idea of hunting is going into the woods, creeping up on a deer, and brushing his fingertips across its fur without it even knowing he was there. Compared to a deer, when it comes to being aware of the world around me, I might as well have headphones on and be listening to Black Sabbath.

"Lockheed wanted to fly on his own. I thought he'd beat me here." I've been watching the skies intermittently ever since I got out of the cab yesterday, but there's been no sign of his little winged self.

"The dragon'll show," Wolverine says confidently. "I did."

I turn to face him. At least he doesn't smell like my Uncle Geoff during Purim anymore. "Big entrance."

"Sorry about that. Wasn't planning it. Sometimes I go off more since…"

"I know." He doesn't have to explain. Her death hit all of us hard. Must be worse for someone who has a short fuse even at the best of times and has convenient blades in his hands. Of course, when the bad guys are coming down on you from every angle, there's no one better to have at your side. So I suppose it all balances out.

He joins me to watch the skies for a time, but it's clear his mind is elsewhere. And then, in seven words, he sum-marizes what it is:

"Super heroes. Summers has gotta be nuts."
Assuming you count "gotta" as one word.
And I can't disagree.

SEVEN

THIS was not remotely what Doctor Rao had had in mind.

When she had confirmed the breakthrough (*her* breakthrough; that was how she had to start thinking of it) to the board, she had assumed that the news would be announced through a dignified press gathering. She had envisioned that the editorial heads of about a half-dozen prestigious scientific journals would gather around the table in one of the conference rooms, and she would present her research to a group of scientifically inclined minds that would be able to understand everything that had gone into the process. Her greatest concern was that they would ask difficult questions, the same questions that some board members were curious about. After her years of research on the topic had come up empty, for instance, how was it she had suddenly had this breakthrough out of nowhere that had exponentially accelerated the entire process? What flash of inspiration had triggered it? She hadn't been exactly evasive with the board, but instead stuck to saying it was really just a set of happenstances, none of them connected, that had prompted her to abruptly pull a lot of pieces together. The board had nodded and congratulated her and agreed with her that the news needed to be announced, preferably through a press conference. Obviously their priorities had been elsewhere: namely, on getting publicity for Benetech.

The prospect of facing a board of formidable scientific journalists had been somewhat daunting. But she needn't have worried. What she was getting was as far a cry from a roundtable of distinguished minds as she could possibly have imagined.

Instead Benetech had rented a small venue off-site at a hotel, one that a number of politicians had used for various announcements, usually because they had accidentally tweeted parts of their anatomy to their mistresses or other such idiocies. The notion of announcing something that could reshape the face of humanity in a room customarily used for such tawdry matters was offensive to her. Almost as offensive as the twenty-year-old woman popping gum while applying makeup to Rao's face as she waited behind the blue curtains for her cue.

"Please take that away," she said to the twenty-year-old, brushing the woman's arm aside. "I'm not going to get any prettier."

"I think you're very pretty," said Tildie, standing next to her. Tildie was a far cry from the terrified child of the other night, but her desperate need for Kavita's support and presence was as palpable as ever. She was clutching Kavita's hand like a drowning girl. The doctor hoped this idiocy wouldn't be too over-whelming for the child.

A thin, slightly twitchy young man named Feist from the publicity department was peering through the curtains. "Doc, you're about to change the world. You gotta look glam!"

"I have to look 'glam'?"

"Yeah! There's gotta be a hundred reporters out there…"

Inwardly Kavita cringed. Outwardly she remained calm. "You know what, Mr. Feist? You should look at photographs of Edison, Einstein, Tesla, Hawking. None of them were especially 'glam,' yet somehow they managed to accomplish what they did without that particular gift. Or is it because I'm a woman? Do you think that if it were a man telling the world what I'm about to tell them, the lead sentence in the news stories would be, 'Dr. Rao took the microphone, looking smashing in a blue Brooks Brothers suit with his hair elegantly coiffed'?"

"Depends on who the reporter is," said Feist.

Despite it all, she allowed a small smile at that. "Perhaps." She glanced down at her young charge, who didn't seem the least bit concerned about what they were about to face. "Are you all right, Tildie? You're not scared?"

"Do I get to sit near you?" That was the only thing that mattered to her. The message was clear. With Kavita at her side, Tildie could face anything, no matter how horrific.

Kavita Rao had known for a long time that she would never be able to have children. A fertilized egg had a better chance of surviving in the Mojave than it did in her uterus. She had not been bothered when she'd received the news. No one understood better than a geneticist that sometimes people simply drew the biological short straw, and that's the way it went. Some people could eat a whole pizza and not gain an ounce; others could eat a slice and pick up two pounds that never went away. Some were tall, some short, some fertile, some…not. No use arguing about it or expending any anguish.

Yet now, with the way Tildie looked at her as if she were the most important person in the world, Kavita felt a tinge of anguish and regret that she would never have a child of her own. That in fact Tildie would likely be the closest she would ever get.

Might as well make the most of it.

"You're going to be standing right next to me, actually. Here's what's going to happen. I'm going to come out and talk to the people out there a little bit first. And then we're going to bring you out so the people can meet you…"

"Are—?" Her voice caught a moment.

"What is it, honey?"

Her voice so soft that Kavita had to strain to hear her, Tildie said, "Are they going to be mad at me? Because of what I did?"

Kavita crouched so she would be eye-to-eye with the child. "No. Because I'm going to explain to them—just as I explained to you—that it wasn't your fault. At all. No one gets mad at you for something that isn't your fault. And I'm going to explain to them why it can never happen again. Mad at you? They're going to be happy for you."

"Really?"

"Really. Oh. I have something for you." She pulled out a small, rectangular object from her bag and held it up.

Tildie's eyes widened and she gasped in delight. "A DS?"

"A DS3," Kavita corrected her. "For you."

Tildie took it and held it almost reverently. "I so wanted one…"

"I know. It's already loaded with some games. And it comes with this…" She jacked in a small set of headphones. "So it won't make noise, you can play it while wearing these. Let's get you set up."

Moments later Tildie was sitting cross-legged on the floor, completely absorbed in a game, headphones nestled comfortably over her ears. Kavita watched her and nodded in satisfaction.

"Showtime, Doc?" said Feist.

She could feel the fight-or-flight reflex kicking in, one of the most basic of survival instincts hardwired into the genetic code. She took a deep breath, eased it out to steady her nerves, and then nodded.

Feist stepped through the curtain and a barrage of flashes went off immediately, as if a miniature lightning storm had erupted in the room. Feist raised his hands and said, "Folks, folks…save it. I'm not the one you're interested in.

"The woman you're about to meet is here to tell you about a discovery that will solve one of the great problems of our current society and, at the same time, improve the quality of life of hundreds of thousands of people. Now, 'hundreds of thousands' may not seem like a particularly large number since well over a quarter of a billion live in this country alone. Nevertheless, considering the nature of the individuals in question, the ramifications will in fact be global in scale. And here, to explain it all to you, please join me in welcoming renowned geneticist Doctor Kavita Rao."

She pushed the curtains aside and stepped out into the light. She had to squint against the intensity of it as she made her way to the podium. There was a darkened monitor screen set up to the right that she would be using shortly. An array of microphones stood in front of her, representing a dozen different news agencies. Feist had been right: There had to be at least a hundred people crammed into the room, recording devices of all sorts aimed at her to take down every word. For some reason she had a quick mental image of a caveman announcing the invention of the wheel while a cave reporter rapidly etched pictures on a nearby wall to immortalize the moment. *Not sure we've really advanced all that much since then.*

Kavita paused at the microphone and gathered her thoughts. Then she launched herself into the void.

"What is a mutant?" she asked, not expecting a response and not receiving one. "They've been called angels and devils. They've committed atrocities and been victims of atrocities themselves. Yes, they've been labeled monsters, and not without reason. But I will tell you what mutants are. Mutants are people. No better or worse by nature than anybody else. Just…people. People with a disease."

She saw a few raised eyebrows from the group. It didn't surprise her. They'd spent years writing about the "mutant menace," egged on by blowhard pundits like that moron who owned *The Daily Bugle*. The notion of lumping in mutants with people who were genuinely struggling with illness didn't seem a comfortable fit with the narrative many of them already had in their heads. Well, she was just going to have to educate them.

"Mutants," she continued, "are not the next step in evolution. They are not the Homo sapiens to our Neanderthals, no matter how many times the term 'Homo superior' might be invoked by certain mutant activists. They are not the end of humankind. The mutant gene is nothing more than a disease. A corruption of healthy cellular activity. And now…at last…we have found a cure."

That statement was enough to rouse the interest of those reporters who had thought this was just going to be some sort of dry recitation, a topic they'd have to labor mightily to make interesting to their readership. Immediately they started to pepper her with questions, which she found somewhat irritating since obviously she had only just begun explaining the facts of the matter to them. She raised her hands to quiet them, and they responded.

"I'm going to show you some video footage now," she said slowly, carefully, as if explaining things to idiots…which, to some degree, they were. "I am warning you now, it is very graphic in nature, and it is only by the merest happenstance that we have it in our possession. This footage was shot for a television program called *Patrol,* in which a videographer is sent on ride-alongs with police officers. The purpose of the program is to show policemen performing their normal, everyday duties. To convey to the viewership how patrols are oftentimes extended tours of boredom, punctuated by occasional unexpected violence. Not to sound melodramatic, but this particular evening, the officers got much more than they bargained for."

The remote control for the video, already set up, was on her podium right where it was supposed to be. She picked it up and activated it. "These particular officers are Raymond Hoyt, whom you'll see on the right, and Lazlo Richards at the wheel."

The screen flared to life. Officer Hoyt was turned around in the driver's seat, addressing the camera. *"We get reports from neighbors all the time. Couple screaming at each other…usually they've had a few drinks. They need to calm down. That's what we're there to accomplish. But they see us and it just, you know…it can be inflammatory. The uniform. Always gotta compensate. Defuse."*

A house was now visible through the windshield of the car. Richards spoke up without looking into the camera. *"Domestics, they're the worst. You never know what you're going to be walking into. Might be a power couple who both had a bad day at the office and all you need to do is talk them down."* Richards contin-

ued talking as they climbed out of the car, his back
still to the camera. *"On the other hand, could be,
y'know, a guy with a rap sheet a mile long who's packing, and suddenly you're in a firefight…"*

They approached the front door, the unseen cameraman still sitting in the car. Suddenly there was a
horrifying scream. High-pitched, female, and this
wasn't simply the sound of a woman being threatened
by a brutal husband. This was someone who knew that
she was facing something—not someone—that was
going to kill her in a matter of seconds. The sort of terrifying sound that seared itself into the brains of the
listeners and would remain there until their dying day.

"God," Richards said.

Hoyt shoved at the front door to no avail and bellowed, *"Back door! Now!"*

They tore around the side of the building while the
cameraman was still stumbling to get out of the vehicle.
Then he was running, the camera bouncing slightly in
the grand tradition of *cinema verite*. He came around the
rear of the house to find the back door wide open, and
then there was another scream, a man this time, sounding just as terrified as the female had been. If anyone
watching the video had thought the husband was about
to murder his wife, they now knew there was far more
than a simple homicide involved.

For just a heartbeat, the camera's point of view
didn't move. It was clear that the cameraman was

hesitating. There was something terrible going on in that house, something that was more than the cameraman was expecting or prepared to deal with, and he was taking a moment to screw up his nerve sufficiently to go inside. Then he finally managed to do so, and the camera point of view followed in the wake of the cops.

Kavita watched with finely honed impassivity. She wasn't bothering to look at the screen. Instead she was watching the news people, seeing them react, bracing themselves for whatever was about to happen. It was clearly going to be really, really bad.

She was very glad she had thought to present Tildie with the video-game device and earphones. Glancing offstage, she saw that it was serving the girl's needs perfectly. Tildie was peacefully playing the game, her earphones blocking out Kavita's video presentation so the girl wouldn't have to be subjected to it again. Nothing was going to be helped if Tildie became a sobbing mess on stage while the visual details of that horrible night were being played out in front of her. The screams, the sounds of tearing flesh, crunching bones, and people in their death throes… why in God's name should she be forced to relive that in excruciating detail?

Then came the collective gasp as what some would call the money shot appeared on the screen. The cameraman had emerged onto the second floor, pushing

open a bedroom door that opened on to hell. Richards stood there, his gun pointed but his hands shaking. A corpse, barely recognizable as a woman, lay
shredded on a queen-sized bed, while a man—pre-
sumably her husband—was being held against a wall,
blood cascading down behind him. On the opposite
wall was the cop that Kavita had identified as Officer
Hoyt. He was similarly pinned, and the creature that
was holding them both...

It was a monster beyond nightmares, beyond horrifying. And the thing that was most surreal of all was
that right in the middle of the creature, just sort of
floating there, was a little girl. Her eyes were closed,
her face covered in shadows, her nightgown drenched
in blood.

The image froze.

"That's all there is," Kavita said calmly. "All
that's directly applicable, anyway. I doubt that
footage of the cameraman running in the opposite
direction while screaming a string of profanities
would be terribly useful."

There was a deathly silence then. Clearly the
people in the room weren't quite sure what they
had just seen.

She turned off the screen, and then made eye
contact with Feist and nodded slightly. Without
drawing attention to himself, he quietly moved offstage to get Tildie. As he did so, Kavita said, "A

child's mutant power usually presents itself at puberty. This was not the case for Tildie Soames. Her ability to manifest her own nightmares cost the lives of her parents as well as Officer Hoyt. She understands—at least now—that this was not her fault. I would appreciate all of you understanding that as well."

Feist escorted a clearly nervous Tildie out onto the stage. She watched the press people warily, and they seemed no less wary of her. Kavita supposed they couldn't be blamed for this, considering what she had just shown them. But she was determined not to let any of this suspicion undermine Tildie's state of mind.

"This brave child," said Kavita, "offered to work with us, under the supervision of her guardians and government health agencies, to test Benetech's new treatment." She put out a hand to Tildie, who came straight to her and, instead of taking the hand, wrapped her arms around Kavita's waist without ever taking her nervous eyes off the cameras. "In the coming months, she will make herself available to genetic teams from every nation to prove what we now conclusively know." She stroked the child's head lovingly. "The mutant strain can be eliminated, safely and irreversibly. There *is* such a thing as a second chance."

EIGHT

"...**AND** although information is scattered and conflicting, we have been able to determine this much: A group of machine-gun-wielding masked gunmen, varying in reports from five to ten in number, have taken over the penthouse of the Chapman Building, where an annual charity party is being hosted by noted patron of the arts Walter Langford. The gunmen attacked the party at approximately 8 p.m. Eastern. Shots were fired, and although it is uncertain whether anyone has been killed, we do know that many are still alive and being held hostage. It is unknown at this time why the hostages have been taken or whether there are to be ransom demands. The Department of Homeland Security has determined that this may well be a terrorist attack, and currently the

FBI has cordoned off a four-block radius. We will be carrying further details live—"

He stands in the middle of the room, the terror-filled faces of his hostages looking up at him. He is watching the news report via the small phone device in his palm, the one that he has taken away from one of the petrified people, and now his huge, armored hand closes around it and crunches it effortlessly. He wipes the bits of destroyed phone off his hands and stares at the people with red eyes. The unhealthy green pallor of his skin, the absence of a nose, the strange piece of metal running across the middle of his face, all combine to tell the hostages that he is not of this world.

Either that or an evil mutant.

His men are all too human, and reveling in the violence. They seemed to have enjoyed firing their weapons in the air, shouting at everyone to get down on the floor, warning them that they'd be happy to put bullets into the brains of anyone who defies them. Idiots, the lot of them, but useful idiots.

Now there is deathly silence as everyone waits for him to speak.

"No doubt you're wondering what it is we want," he says, his voice soft but accompanied by a deep rumbling, like a slowly moving avalanche. "Your money. Your daughters. Your flesh, peeled

and roasted. Maybe we're fanatics. Or maybe…
we're just bored.

"In point of fact…I'm not going to tell you. Not
yet. But trust me:

"You'll know it when you see it."

Calm before the storm. That's what this feels like.

I try not to look at Emma as we both change out of our clothes. Although with her, it's hard to tell when she's dressed and undressed; there's so little difference.

I know we're both women. I know we're both mutants. But as we change in total quiet, sometimes I find it hard to believe that we're even the same species.

The costume is waiting for me in my locker. I hold it up. It's not bad, actually. Not as bad as I thought it would be. I like the combination of blue and yellow. It's old-school, in every sense.

I dress quickly, because being naked in front of Emma Frost makes me feel incredibly vulnerable. I zip up the front, snap shut the belt, pull on the boots. There's no mirrors in here, but what I can see looks pretty damned nice.

I turn around. Emma is sporting one of her standard, slutted-up white outfits. How come *she* doesn't have to wear a new team costume? What, she's not good enough to be one of us?

Then I realize: no. She's not. And I'm actually fine with that. Scott's trying to take this team in a particular direction, and if she wants to stand alone, like the cheese, separating herself from the rest of us, then that's aces.

THE Beast carefully placed his glasses in their case and clicked it shut. He remembered Emma's comment about how the glasses completely concealed his true identity. She'd been speaking facetiously, of course, but there was something to that. He really did feel like a totally different person when he was wearing them. Refined, cultured, intelligent…the person he truly was inside. It was so easy to overlook that when one stared at him. Inside he was Henry McCoy.

On the outside…

On the outside, the best-case scenarios had snickering students referring to him behind his back as Grover, another blue furry monster. He wanted to see that as a term of endearment, perhaps. Really, who didn't love Grover? Certainly it was better than Elmo, that insufferably squeaky-voiced, pronoun-challenged red furry sock.

But then there were the others, which pretty much included anyone who didn't live in the mansion.

Scott doesn't know what he's asking of me, Hank thought grimly as he closed the locker door. *He has no clue. Asking me to endure the stares, the flinching, the people turning away. The people who think I'm contagious; if I breathe on them, they might turn into me.*

Although…there was that little girl…

He remembered the time he'd been in Washington, D.C., called in to meet with a senator who was quite the advanced thinker. The senator wanted to propose an amendment that would make assaulting a mutant an official hate crime. Beating up on a mutant, no matter how harmless he or she might be, currently got you lauded by all your pals. Under the new amendment, you'd be looking at not only jail time for assault and battery, but also additional time for selecting a mutant as your target. The senator wanted Hank's scientific input as to the nature of mutation in general.

So Hank had met with him, answered all his questions, and aided him in framing the language so that if heroes such as the X-Men were battling an evil mutant who was involved in hatching some scheme, they wouldn't themselves be subject to legal penalties.

"We're going to change the face of the law with this," the senator had said. After leaving his office, Hank had gone to a park and just sat there, enjoying the sun. Then he'd looked down as a pig-tailed little girl, not more than two years old, wandered up to him, and—looking up at him with round, amazed eyes—

cooed, "Kitty!" Apparently she had mistaken him for the large blue-furred protagonist from *Monsters, Inc.* The child's mother came running up, terrified, but all Hank did was laugh heartily and tell the child he'd say "hi" to Mike Wazowski for her. She promptly threw her arms around his leg and said, "kitty" once more. A furred hand that could rip an enemy to shreds patted her gently on the head, and the mother looked both relieved and fascinated. Hank chatted with her for a minute or two, and it turned out she was a neurobiologist who was familiar with his name. When they had to leave, the little girl waved and the mother said, "Pleasure meeting you."

He'd wanted to sob with joy. Such a simple thing: *Pleasure meeting you.* It had meant the world to him.

That had been a good day. That had been a very good day.

Three weeks later the senator had proposed the amendment on the floor of the Senate. Usually, no one watched C-Span. This time everyone did. The video went viral. Pundits from both sides pummeled the senator relentlessly for weeks. The bill died in committee, and the following year, with his opposition playing the video in an endless loop of commercials and tagging him as being "soft on the mutant menace," he was voted out of office by the largest margin in state history. A third-party candidate, who asserted that he was running because Martians had told him to, actually polled higher.

Hank had gotten uncharacteristically drunk that night, watching the returns as they came in. He hadn't gone on to pick a fight with anyone; he was a quiet drunk. He just sat there smoldering.

The entire business had taught Hank the danger of hope.

Yet now Scott was suggesting they throw themselves into the hellhole of public opinion of their own free will. Try to change the perception of mutants in the eyes of people who—Hank couldn't help but note—could still throw rocks and bricks at them or maybe string one of them up, without having it considered a hate crime. Because to many, the only good mutant remained a dead mutant, and the law was okay with that.

He crouched for a moment, overwhelmed by the possibility that this was an exercise in hubris at its worst, thinking that a handful of mutants could possibly shift public opinion about their kind. It was absurd. How could anyone with a logical mind think the citizenry as a whole would ever see him, in particular, as anything other than a dangerous furry monster, a berserk gorilla wandering in their midst?

And that was when the words of Margaret Mead, noted anthropologist, sprang into his mind unbidden.

Never doubt that a small group of thoughtful, committed citizens can change the world. Indeed, it is the only thing that ever has.

He took one last look at his glasses case, said, "This one's for you, Maggie," closed the locker door, and headed out.

WOLVERINE sat in his room, staring at the new costume.

And staring at it.

And staring at it.

"Yeah, okay," he said, and put it on. Once he had done so, he popped his claws once to make sure that the sheathes on his gloves were lined up. Then he pulled on the mask, muttered, "I gotta be outta my mind," and headed down to the landing bay.

CYCLOPS was already in the landing bay when they arrived. The Blackbird was likewise waiting for them, displaying exactly as much emotion as Cyclops was. He looked them up and down once, and the only reason they knew that—since they had no clear view of his eyes—was that his head tilted slightly.

"Time to make nice with the public, eh, Summers?"

"We have to do more than that, Logan," Cyclops said firmly, with the confidence of a true zealot. Like something out of *The Right Stuff,* his teammates walked on either side of him as he headed toward the

Blackbird. "We have to astonish them."

Minutes later the Blackbird launched into the night air.

EDWARD Tancredi despised his name, because his nickname "Eddie" rhymed with his last name. He was a slender, blond-haired young man who tended to walk with an extremely light footfall. It was a tendency he'd developed since his mutant power, the ability to fly, had first manifested. Originally he had thought that in this school where so many bizarre and interesting powers existed, simply being able to take wing wouldn't seem like such a big deal. But on the first day, when he'd soared over the top of the school to get a better feel for the lay of the place, he'd seen so many land-bound students looking up at him with clear envy that he'd felt better about it. If nothing else, in real-world terms, never having to worry about traffic jams for the rest of his life was a pretty sweet deal.

And when he'd seen a portrait of the original X-Men in a place of honor, and saw a guy with wings in the forefront, it had even made him feel a kinship to the school's founders.

As a result, he'd come to conclude that flight was totally *the* power that all the baddest of the good guys had.

Edward was walking down a hallway when the glass of a nearby window began to rattle. He stopped and looked out, squinting into the darkening sky, and then he saw it: the Blackbird, heading off into the night, the X-Men inside doubtless planning to go head-to-head with the forces of whatever.

"God, I love this school," he said.

There was a clatter of footsteps down the hallway. Moments later, Hisako Ichiki was sprinting toward him. Hisako had charmed him right from the get-go, mostly because she seemed reluctant to make any sort of eye contact. Whenever she spoke to him, she looked down at her shoes or off to the side. He didn't know why he thought that was cute, but he did. She wasn't exactly his type—he tended to lust after tall, willowy blondes, and the diminutive Japanese girl was hardly that. Not that he'd had any luck in the tall, willowy blonde department, but a guy could dream, couldn't he? Currently his dreams tended to focus around the three identical blondes known collectively as the Stepford Cuckoos. He wasn't sure what their deal was, except they were telepaths who tended to finish each other's sentences, they looked a lot like teenage versions of Emma Frost, and there were rumors they were actually clones of her. Their names were Celeste, Mindee, and Phoebe, and he couldn't tell any one apart from the other. He wondered if they were even able to operate separately from each other, which led him to think he had little to no chance with even one of them…

But…maybe all three…?

"Are you all right?" Hisako asked him. "You suddenly started sweating. A lot."

"Fine. I'm fine," he said hurriedly.

Edward and Hisako had first "connected" when the Sentinel-illusion had attacked them. While the other students were freaking out, Edward had gained elevation to try to figure out what was going on, and Hisako had surrounded herself with a kind of psionic body armor that Edward had subsequently told her was "totally sick." This had concerned her until he'd explained that was a positive thing…like "ill." At which point she had said it was no wonder she didn't understand health-care debates in this country since she didn't even understand the words anymore. He had laughed at that, and a friendship was born.

He jabbed a thumb out the window toward the rapidly dwindling Blackbird and said, "Hey, check it out—"

"Eddie, did you hear?" she said urgently.

"How could I not hear?" he replied. "That thing makes one hellacious racket when it takes off…"

"What?" She looked confused. "No, not that. I mean about the cure."

"What? They're doing a concert in town?"

"Not *The* Cure. The cure! A cure!"

"You lost me. A cure for what?"

"For us!"

"Are we sick?"

Her face darkened. "That's what they're saying. They're talking about it downstairs. It's on all the news channels. It's on everything. Come on," and she grabbed him by the wrist and yanked him literally off his feet. She pulled him like a blond-haired balloon, and he floated along behind her.

Moments later he was sitting in front of the wide-screen television in the den, surrounded by dozens of other students. Learning that they were all ill. Learning that there was a cure for that illness. Learning that the mutant menace could finally be eliminated for all time.

The news stations had all switched away from what was happening at the Chapman building. That ongoing story had been reduced to a tiny crawl of a headline across the bottom of the screen. After all, what did it matter what a handful of terrorists were doing to a bunch of the one percent in a fancy warehouse? This was a story about ending one of the greatest threats humanity had ever faced. Who cared about anything else?

"WHAT do we see?" Cyclops asked.

The conversation in the Blackbird had been minimal during the short flight into Manhattan. Everyone had been lost in their own thoughts. Cyclops was at the helm, while Beast's fingers worked the scanning devices with surprising lightness.

"Scanner's reading about thirty-five warm bodies in the penthouse, six of them carrying something a lot warmer," said Beast briskly.

"Bombs?"

"Or guns. State-of-the-Art-of-War." Trust the Beast to make a pun off a still-popular text written centuries ago. He paused, then added, "Wasn't S.H.I.E.L.D. developing some kind of thermal ordnance?"

Wolverine stuck his head in, literally. "These clowns ain't S.H.I.E.L.D.," he said.

Cyclops was willing to defer to Wolverine's opinion on that. Wolverine had had far more interaction with the notoriously close-to-the-vest espionage organization, particularly its legendary eyepatched leader, Nick Fury. Wolverine tapped the thermal readout on the screen of Beast's array. "Deployment's amateur hour. Right flank's wide open. That's your entry point."

"Maybe," Cyclops said guardedly, not wanting to commit to an attack plan until he was sure he had all the bases covered. They were on dangerous ground, after all, and not just from the gun-wielding lunatics. The problem with launching an assault in the public eye for the purpose of burnishing one's image was that, if it all went south and the X-Men wound up with a few dozen corpses on their hands, they were the ones who were going to be blamed by Joe and Jane Average Citizen sitting in front of their TV screens. Not the bad guys. Them. "Our biggest question mark's the hostages. If any of them get it in their heads to play hero, we could have a problem."

"The hostages," Emma said, gazing down at the scene, "are flat on the ground praying or peeing."

Even Kitty seemed impressed. "You can read them from here?"

"I don't have to. This is Walter Langford's annual fundraiser for the preservation of Victorian architecture. I know their type. Raised in privilege, unaccustomed to doing anything on their own. They might order their butlers and maids into a fight, but they won't lift a finger to save themselves. They're sheep."

"How do you know them so well?"

"Because I used to be one of the shepherds," Emma said, her mouth twitching slightly. "It's the first year I've missed it."

"Then why ain't'cha down there right now?" said Wolverine.

She looked at him with cold amusement. "Apparently my invitation got lost in the mail."

He was quiet for a moment, then said, "Sucks when that happens."

"Indeed."

"Yeah. Missed the recent royal wedding because of it."

"The queen asked after you, if that's any consolation," Emma assured him.

Beast ignored the sarcastic exchange. "Our biggest question isn't the hostages or the men with the bright and beautiful weaponry. Our biggest question," and he pointed toward a large blue circle in the middle of his screen, "is that."

"Who is that?" said Wolverine

"The readings don't line up with anything human or, for that matter, anything in our database. The question isn't 'who' so much as 'what.'"

NINE

———————— 🪐 ————————

HILLARY Masterson was terrified for her child.

She didn't know what her child looked like, or would sound like, or what its name would be, or even its gender. She hadn't gone to the doctor yet, although she'd made an appointment.

The only thing she knew for sure was that her baby needed to be born and grow up and cure cancer while running a successful presidential campaign and winning a Nobel Peace Prize for Everything.

All this because Hillary had peed on a stick that morning, and when it had come up positive, her world had reoriented itself.

She'd been overjoyed.

She hadn't told Brad yet. He'd been called away to a meeting in Tokyo the day before. So she was going to wait to tell him in person. She was anxious to see the look on his tanned, mustached face. He was such a sentimentalist, he probably wouldn't know whether to laugh or cry and would likely wind up doing both.

All of that had gone through her head that morning as she danced around the bedroom, tossing off her nightgown and pirouetting about, totally nude and filled with joy.

The day had hurtled past her. She'd gone to the hairdresser to get spiffed up for Wally Langford's bash that evening, and she thanked her lucky stars she'd taken the test that morning because she knew not to drink that night. Which was a killer, because Wally didn't skimp when it came to the quality of the liquor.

Then Hillary had slithered into a floor-length green sheathe dress, the kind she wouldn't be able to wear by her second trimester, but that was all right. It would be *so* last season within two months anyway.

She'd gone to the party hoping she would be able to contain herself, because nobody, absolutely nobody could find out before Brad. Yet Rosa Lee Tepper eyed her *most* curiously when Hillary passed on a nice Bordeaux in favor of ginger ale, and wasn't buying for a moment Hillary's contention that she had an upset stomach. "You could be bleeding out your eyeballs and still not refuse a Bordeaux," Rosa Lee said suspiciously. "What's going on?"

Please let there be a distraction right now, Hillary thought desperately.

That was when the men had shown up. The horrible, swaggering, snarling, dangerous men, covered head to toe in black with masks on, wielding huge guns that they fired into the air, demanding that everybody hit the floor. Rich people, filthy rich people in their designer gowns and tailored suits, flopping down like fish, shaking in terror, mewling, pleading. People who could buy yachts with money out of petty cash were no braver in the face of these lethal men than the poorest of ditch diggers would have been. These people who thought they ruled the world because of who they were, as if their money made them more special than anyone else. It was hard to dwell on one's position in society when that position was on the floor.

Hillary had gotten her distraction. And now there was a great likelihood her baby was going to die before it ever had a chance to live.

She lay on the floor, curled up in a fetal position that would provide as much protection for her child as possible. On some level it was a pointless exercise; if she were killed, it wasn't as if they could save the infant. It existed as nothing more than a plus sign on a stick and in an extended imaginary life in Hillary's head.

The behemoth leader of the men who had broken into the party was standing dead center of the room.

Hillary had no idea what to make of him. She'd read about horrible creatures like this: Some of them had been transformed by radiation, some of them came from the stars, and still others were actually born that way. "Mutants," those ones were called. Fearsome, grotesque, corrupted and deformed shadows of human beings. There were rumors that anyone could be a mutant: "The Terror That Could Be Living Next Door," one newspaper had put it. But she didn't believe that. Certainly if they looked like the monstrosity terrorizing this group, they wouldn't be allowed in *any* of the better neighborhoods.

He was looking upward, this monster, as if he could see straight through the ceiling. "Hmmm," he muttered. "A moth. A single moth would have made more noise touching down." Then he raised his voice slightly, apparently to make sure his men heard him. "Company's here."

"Bring 'em on, baby!" said one of his men. Another stroked his gun like a woman and declared, "We are locked and loaded. Heartbreakers and life takers, am I right?"

"Oh, yeah!" shouted one of his pals.

"Bring on the muties!"

"Oh, *yeah!*"

"Are you finished?" asked the monster.

We're going to die, Hillary said to herself, losing her final hope. *Everything I read, everything I've heard, it's all true. This monster is a mutant and other mutants are going to show up, and they're going to kill us all, my baby…I should have told Rosa Lee. I should have shared it with someone…*

Her gaze shifted toward Rosa Lee, the woman whose curiosity had caused Hillary to wish, however inadvertently, for this nightmare that had descended upon them.

Rosa Lee wasn't there.

That was the damnedest thing.

Hillary could have sworn that Rosa Lee was lying directly across from her. There was no way she could have gotten out. Even the slightest movement would have been noticed, much less an all-out escape. Yet she was gone. How could that possibly—?

The sudden chatter of gunfire caused Hillary to cry out and cover her ears, drawing her knees up even more tightly toward her stomach. No one heard her because everyone else was screaming as well, and combined with all of that were the howls of the masked man who was emptying his gun into the nearby windows. Glass shattered and fell everywhere. He was bellowing, *"Thought I didn't see you, huh! Thought you'd sneak by!"*

"Soldier!" shouted the strange, monstrous leader. Amazingly his voice soared above all of the shrieking and even the sounds of the bullets. The man in black stopped shooting. Hillary dared to peek out from un-

der her arm and saw there was still a crazed look on his face, his blue eyes wide with fury, and…

Wait a minute. What the hell—?

Leon Brisbane was gone. And Candy Hardacy. And Rachel McClaren, and Hubert Perkins, and Walter himself. She wasn't imagining it. The guests were disappearing.

And the leader hadn't noticed, distracted as he was by the crazed soldier who stood there with smoke wafting out the muzzle of the barrel. "Who," said the monstrous leader, "are you talking to?"

The masked man turned to the leader. The mask had large eyeholes cut out and a wide space for his mouth, so it was obvious he was looking at the leader with an air of incredulity.

The masked man turned, looked at the shattered window, and then back to the leader. The demented fervor was dissipating from his face, like someone awakening from a walking dream. Even as he made the reply, it was clear he was realizing it made no sense whatsoever. "My, uh…my swim coach. I swore if I ever saw him…and I did…and he went flying right back through the window, just like I always imagined."

The answer was completely nonsensical. It was ridiculous. A figure from—what? High school? Had returned to torment him out of the blue? It was insane.

Yet the leader didn't seem the slightest bit disturbed about it. Instead he actually gave a little nod, as if this were the most natural thing in the world. "Miss Frost is here," he announced, a name that meant nothing to Hillary. "Turn up your scramblers and keep her out of your heads. Go hot on weapons. This will happen fast."

What? What's going to happen fast…?

Suddenly a yellow-gloved hand clamped over Hillary's mouth. She gasped in surprise but the hand muffled the sound, and suddenly she felt a bizarre tingling. The floor was starting to rise around her…

No. No, she was sinking. Sinking *into* the floor. Then she was surrounded by blackness for maybe half a second.

And then she was back out, out into the light, and she fell lightly into a room. It was an office by the looks of it, a big fancy office like the senior partner in a law firm might use. She thudded to the floor, landing on her rump.

A young woman who couldn't have been more than twenty stood there, clad in blue and yellow. She was pointing with urgency toward the door at the far end. "Get going. Use the stairs; the electrical systems may get knocked out. The others I rescued are already on their way out. Move it."

"Are…are *you* a *mutant*?"

"Yes. Now go." The young woman was actually starting to float up toward the ceiling again, as if walking on the very molecules of the air.

And having no idea why, Hillary blurted out, "I'm pregnant."

The mutant girl stopped for a moment and stared.

"I'm sorry," said Hillary, "I…just wanted to tell someone."

With great gravity, the mutant girl said "*Mazel tov.*" Then she disappeared into the ceiling.

Hunh. I wonder if all mutants are Jewish, she thought as she sprinted out of the room. It occurred to her that, if mutants could look like that, it was entirely possible that some of her neighbors *were* in fact mutants.

Which was no longer such a threatening concept to her.

Then she heard all hell break loose on the floor above. But she didn't hang around to see it.

THE soldier—the one who was positive that somehow he had just managed to shred his swimming coach—was still staring out the window when the Beast swung through feet first, gripping firmly on to the edge of the roof overhead. The Beast's blue-furred feet took the soldier solidly in the gut, driving him upward. He crashed into the tiled ceiling, knocking the air out of him, his head slamming hard into its surface. The Beast then swung back in the other direction, allowing the soldier to tumble to the floor.

Another soldier turned and brought his gun around, ready to open fire on the fast-moving, animalistic mutant. He never got the opportunity. The wall next to him suddenly exploded, blown open by a powerful red force beam that nothing could have resisted. He was unconscious before he hit the ground.

Cyclops stepped through. A third soldier, standing off to the right beyond the mutant leader's peripheral vision, had a clear shot and took aim immediately. He was so focused on Cyclops that he didn't see Emma Frost stride forward. On the outside, she was no longer mere flesh and blood. She had instead employed her secondary ability, which she typically favored when going into a combat situation: Her body had transformed into an organic form of glittering diamond. It provided her both a high degree of invulnerability and also increased strength. As casually as if she were hailing a taxi—something Emma would never be caught dead doing—she stuck out her left arm and clotheslined the soldier. The blow struck him across the throat and he coughed up blood as his rifle went flying.

A fourth soldier didn't know where to look first: left, right, in front of or behind him. While he was trying to make up his mind, Wolverine cut through the ceiling with his claws and crashed down from overhead. The soldier looked up, and then he wasn't looking at anything. Wolverine had knocked him cold, an action for which he should have been grateful. Wolverine could just as easily have taken his head off.

Meanwhile Kitty continued to pop up and down through the floor like a ghostly mutant Whac-a-mole, pulling one hostage after another to safety. There was still a handful of tuxedoed men remaining when the X-Men converged from all sides on the leader, who was essentially the eight hundred pound gorilla in the room. Kitty fully materialized in the room, hoping—praying—that the fight was more or less over. The X-Men had just dismantled all the black-clad guys within seconds. Certainly this one creature wasn't going to try to stand alone against them.

"Hmm," he said, not sounding particularly perturbed at being alone and surrounded. "X-Men...you do not disappoint."

"This doesn't have to go any further," Cyclops warned him.

He snorted. It sounded as if it was supposed to be a laugh of some sort. "I wasn't aware it had begun."

"Whatever it is you want from these people..."

"He got it already, Cyclops," said Wolverine. "This was a test."

The behemoth nodded slightly. "Not a difficult one, it's true. But you still performed admirably." He glanced at Emma and added, almost as an afterthought, "And don't meddle with my mind, Miss Frost. You could not hope to decipher my thoughts.

Whereas yours…"

And suddenly there was some sort of round device in his hand. It looked like the Chinese weapon called a wind and fire wheel. It was a flat, metal ring with long, vicious blades extending from the edges, like fangs, clearly capable of slicing anyone they struck to ribbons. The behemoth gripped the blade tightly by its handle, and it was suddenly obvious he had no intention of surrendering.

Without a word spoken between them, but moving simultaneously due to long practice, Wolverine and Cyclops went for him from either side. Cyclops unleashed an optic blast as Wolverine leaped through the air, ready to hit hard and fast with his claws. Before the blast could strike home, the behemoth brought his armored right arm up and deflected it effortlessly.

Kitty tried to shout a warning that there were still hostages about. She wanted to cry out that if everyone could just keep their testosterone in check for another minute or so, she could get the remaining hostages to safety—since it was obvious that the big guy wasn't really interested in them—and then the combatants could proceed to beat the living crap out of each other in relative peace. She didn't have the opportunity, however, as the deflected optic blast hit her broadside and knocked her off her feet. She lay on the ground, stunned, barely managing to remain conscious.

The huge being spun out of the way of Wolverine's attack, which wouldn't have seemed possible given his size. He drove his left fist forward, catching the clawed mutant squarely on the chin. Wolverine's head snapped back, momentarily staggering him. Pressing his attack, the behemoth swung the wind and fire wheel. It sliced directly across Wolverine's gut. He went down, clutching at his stomach, trying not to think about what it was he was shoving back into place while waiting for his healing factor to return him to fighting condition.

The behemoth sensed something coming in fast behind him and tried to turn to face it. This time he was too slow, and the hurtling Beast slammed into him from behind. The Beast struck the behemoth repeatedly in the side of the head and the upper shoulders, snarling in a voice not remotely recognizable as human.

Across the room, Cyclops was taking aim, waiting for a clear shot. The behemoth didn't give the Beast time to provide one. Instead he charged directly at Cyclops, with the struggling Beast still atop him. Then he leaped up, hurtling straight toward the team's leader while twisting around in midair so the Beast would take the brunt of the impact. The strategy worked. Cyclops didn't dare fire lest he hit his furred ally, and he wasn't fast enough to get out of the way. The three of them collided, Cyclops hitting the floor first, with the Beast crunched between Cyclops on the ground and the behemoth atop him.

The X-Men's adversary started to get to his feet, and something remarkably solid suddenly struck him in the face.

Emma Frost came in fast and hard, maintaining her impervious diamond form. She battered him quickly, repeatedly, her fists flashing, her body gleaming in the light from the overhead lamps.

Yet despite her incessant pounding, the behemoth managed to get to his feet and, upon doing so, grabbed her by the throat. Her eyes widened in astonishment, unable to fathom how in the world he had endured so much punishment at her hands without showing the slightest sign of damage.

"Diamond," he snarled with contempt. Keeping one massive hand firmly on Emma's throat, he reached out with his other hand and snared her ankle. "I am Ord of the Breakworld. We stuff our pillows with diamonds."

And with that, he slammed Emma to the floor with such force that she went straight through it, waving her arms helplessly as she crashed down into the suite of offices below.

The self-identified Ord of the Breakworld turned to face his erstwhile opponents, blood dripping from his weapon. "I was wrong. I *am* disappointed. The mighty X-Men. And not one of them strong enough to—"

Something fluttered in the air just behind him. He turned, his face a question. "Wait—"

His assailant didn't wait.

The next thing Ord knew, he was under attack by what could only be described as a dragon. Three feet long from tip of nose to tip of tail, purple-skinned with flapping wings on its back. When the dragon opened his mouth—which was exactly six inches away from Ord's face—he belched out a massive blast of fire, which so thoroughly consumed Ord's entire head that witnesses would later claim the party had been attacked by Ghost Rider.

Ord screamed. He charged toward a window, batting at his own head, but the fire continued to blaze around his skull as if it had a life of its own. Without slowing down he crashed straight through the window—one of the few that had remained intact during the proceedings—and arced through the sky like a shooting star. It was impossible to determine whether he actually possessed a natural power of flight or if he had some sort of mechanism to propel him through the night sky.

All that really mattered, though, was that he was gone, and the X-Men would live to fight another day. In their line of work, that was always the baseline for a mission's success, much like the old saying that any landing you could walk away from was a good one.

His mouth still steaming, the dragon angled toward Kitty, who—still on the ground, recovering from the impact of the blast—nevertheless spread her arms out in joyous welcome. "Lockheed! You found me! You are the best X-dragon ever!" Lockheed settled onto her torso and she wrapped her arms around him.

Wolverine was still on his knees, his arms crisscrossed over his midsection. "Hell, I think we should make him team leader," he said through gritted teeth. He looked down and saw, through the shredded cloth of his costume, a crimson line across his stomach. It was still tender, and the deep red color of it was awful to look at. Fortunately everything that was supposed to be inside that dark line was properly situated. He knew from long experience that within minutes the deep red would fade to light pink, and then there would be no remaining sign of the gaping hole in his gut.

Cyclops was at the window, watching the last flaming traces of Ord's abrupt departure. "Looks like our friend's gone."

The Beast sounded disappointed, even chiding. "Without so much as a 'This isn't over!' There's simply no etiquette these days as far as villains are concerned. Well...except for Doctor Doofenshmirtz. Not terribly competent, I'll grant you, but 'Curse you, Perry the Platypus' is a keeper of an exit line."

"Would it bother you to know that I've *no* idea what you're talking about?" said Cyclops.

"It would not only *not* bother me, but I'd be astounded if you *did*. And speaking of not knowing things: 'Ord of the Breakworld.' Either of those proper names ring a bell with anyone?"

There were mutual shakings of heads, although Kitty—who had managed to find the strength to sit up—commented, "It's not on the Avengers' list of known alien worlds."

"How do you know?" said Scott.

"I was starved for reading material one day, so I hacked into their database and read it."

"You read and memorized their *entire database?*"

"Only the things that looked interesting."

The Beast gave a low, impressed whistle, and Emma—who had transformed back into her more human-looking body—said in all seriousness, "I know I rarely show it, Katherine, but there are times that I'm relieved you're on *our* side."

Kitty obviously couldn't bring herself to say "thanks," but she nodded in acknowledgment as she got to her feet.

Cyclops glanced around at the remaining civilians, who were still hugging the floor, looking up at them nervously. They seemed to be wondering whether the X-Men were going to beat up on them for a while since the mutants' other target had fled. Inwardly Cyclops sighed; this reordering of their public image was obviously going to take a while. "You can all get up. The danger's over."

Kitty, with Lockheed still perched on her shoulder, reached down and helped a dowager to her feet, a woman with close-cropped, silver hair, a red evening gown, and enough pearls around her neck to sink the *Bismarck.* The woman seemed entranced by Lockheed, and she said to Kitty, "You were *very* brave, my dear."

"Thank you," said Kitty.

"You know, you look like a young Sigourney Weaver."

"I get that a lot."

Okay, well, at least the woman isn't screaming at Kitty to get away from her, so that's something. It was against his nature for Cyclops to look at the positive side of things, but the situation was compelling him to do so. "Zero casualties, which is good," he said to Hank. Then his natural dourness took over. "But any way you slice it, we just got trashed."

He walked to one of the shattered windows and stared down forty stories to street level. The cops had set up spotlights and were flashing them everywhere, trying to get a clearer view of what was going on up in the penthouse. Barricades had been set up to keep people at bay, and even from this distance, Cyclops could see people he took to be police officials conferencing, trying to determine what had transpired and what their next move should be. Former hostages who had been rescued by the X-Men were down there as well, obviously telling the cops their view of what had happened. Cyclops could only hope that his team was coming out positively in the narrative.

He turned back to the X-Men and, in a slightly louder voice, announced, "So now let's do the hard part."

Minutes later they emerged from the front of the building. The people Kitty had already freed from the danger zone were all babbling at once to the police, the press, anyone who would listen. And from what Cyclops could make out from the babbling, everything they were saying was pretty much positive. *Hell, this might work after all.*

The moment they came into view, the questions from the press started flying, fast and furious. The police tried to shout over the tumult, yelling to everyone to back off and allow them to do their job. The gray-haired woman with Kitty called out with a volume that an opera star would have envied, drowning out the orders being barked by the cops. "*These people did your job for you!*" she announced in a voice dripping with breeding and pearls. "*So perhaps* you *are the ones who should be backing off.*"

Meanwhile the press continued pelting the X-Men with questions. "What happened up there?" "Is anybody hurt?" "Was this another mutant attack?"

Cyclops put his hands up to try to silence the reporters so he could address their questions, but they didn't stop shouting them. He realized that all he could do was throw out answers like water balloons and hope some of them soaked in. "Everybody's fine, and no, this is not mutant-related."

"Then why are *you* here?"

Well, there it is, isn't it? I was right. It literally doesn't occur to them that we could be here simply as Samaritans. Time to educate them.

"We came because people were in trouble," he said, as if it were the most obvious thing in the world. So obvious no one should even have to ask about it, but he would condescend to answer all the same. "We X-Men have always felt it is our duty to use our gifts to help not just our own community, but—"

He was on a roll, ready to make all the salient points that had been rattling around in his head.

Naturally the reporters stopped listening, plunging forward with their barrage of questions.

Meanwhile a short, older man, his bow tie askew, sweat beading on his bald pate, was trying to slip through the crowd without being noticed. He didn't succeed. A voice said sharply behind him, *"Mister* Langford."

It brought him up short, and his bow tie bobbed up and down in tandem with his nervous Adam's Apple. "My, uh…my dear Emma. How, uh…how pleasant you were able to make it…"

"Really." Emma stepped in close to him, speaking in a voice so low no one else around could hear her. "I cannot help but notice that your foundations and interests have benefited from my family's *extremely* generous support for many generations. And the very year it becomes public knowledge that I am a mutant, I am—for the first time—left off the guest list. Tell me, *Mister* Langford…would you like to spend the rest of your life obsessed with the works of Leroy Neiman? I mean…sexually?"

He gulped even more, as if he were gasping for air. "I…uh…no. That would be…no, I wouldn't. It was… Emma, it was purely an oversight."

"Oh, I think your sight was fairly clear when you did it. But if that's the story you want to stick with—with the understanding that I could pluck the truth out of your little brain like a raisin out of pudding—then it's my feeling you had better spend the next day or so thinking *very* hard about how you're going to be making this up to me. Do we understand each other, Mister Langford?"

"Ab…" He cleared his throat. "Absolutely. And please, call me 'Walter.'"

"All right. And you can call me 'Miss Frost.'" She turned away from him with a swirl of her white cape.

Cyclops was still trying to sort out one reporter's question from another.

"Will you be charging the city for your services?"

"Will the taxpayers have to cover your fees?" "Are you aware the Avengers do these things for free?" "Are you American citizens and are you willing to provide your birth certificates?" "If it wasn't a mutant, then who led the attack?"

Cyclops seized on the last question he heard. "We don't yet know who attacked..."

"We heard shooting! Did you start the shooting?"

Beginning to feel irritated, Kitty suggested, "Why don't you ask the people we saved what happened?"

"Who flew away?" "Was that Storm?"

Kitty gave the questioner an incredulous look. "Oh, please! Did it *look* like Storm?"

"What are you called, Miss?"

Cyclops was about to warn Kitty off. But then he remembered that he wanted her to serve as the public, non-threatening face of the X-Men. He took a step back to allow her to field questions, hoping she would have better luck than he had.

"Uh, well..." Kitty seemed a bit thrown by the question. "I...mostly 'Shadowcat' is what I used to—"

"Do you have a license for that bat?" They pointed at Lockheed. "What is your relationship with the bat?"

The Beast and Wolverine were standing off to the side. "I bet right now she'd like a bat to smack them in the head with," said Wolverine.

The Beast nodded slightly. As the reporters continued to ask skeptical questions, he sang in a low voice, "You can seeee by our outfits that we are all heeeroes…"

Wolverine grimaced. "Being hated and feared by a world that doesn't understand us beats this circus any day."

"Oh, you're always so grouchy when you get cut in half."

"Doctor McCoy," one of the reporters said, "do you have any comment on this so-called 'mutant cure'?"

Wolverine and the Beast exchanged confused looks. "I'm sorry. 'Cure?'"

"Yes." The reporter, a burly man, pushed his way forward slightly and continued, "Doctor Anita Rhodes from Benetech claimed at a press conference today that she had a cure for the disease that causes people to become mutants…"

"*Disease!*" Wolverine snarled. His hands trembled with fury; it was clear that he was fighting to keep his claws from snapping out. Video of Wolverine disemboweling a reporter wouldn't exactly help with Cyclops' plan for reforming their public image.

The Beast put a quick hand on Wolverine's arm to steady him. "I'm sorry, I have no idea what you're talking about. I've never heard of any…" Then something suddenly clicked into place. "Wait…are you talking about Kavita Rao? Doctor Kavita Rao?"

"Right, right, that's it," said the reporter. "Are you familiar with her work? Do you believe this is the genuine item? Would you make use of it?"

"Oh, we'd use it, awright," said Wolverine. "We'd use it to shove it up her—"

"No comment," the Beast said quickly, overriding Wolverine. "We have no comment at this time. Thank you. Wolverine," and he indicated with a nod of his head that Wolverine should follow him. It was a crapshoot whether Wolverine would do so, and the Beast breathed an inward sigh of relief as Wolverine indulged him.

Cyclops and Kitty were still vainly trying to field questions while Emma just looked on imperiously. Coming in close behind Cyclops, the Beast said in a low voice, "We have to leave. Right now."

"What? Why?"

"Something's come up. I've already been asked about it and my guess is that within thirty seconds or so, you will be, too. And we don't need footage of all of us standing there with stunned expressions saying, 'What are you talking about?'"

"Hank, I don't—"

"A geneticist that I've known for years—Kavita Rao of Benetech—claims that she's invented a cure for that terrible disease called being a mutant."

"What are you talking about?" Cyclops said, stunned.

"See?"

Cyclops didn't hesitate, calling in a loud voice that interrupted Kitty's attempt to explain just what it was that was sitting on her shoulder. "Thank you very much for your questions, ladies and gentlemen. We have to take off, and I mean that literally."

He headed back into the building and, taking his cue, the others started to follow. At which point the ranking police officer on the scene shouted, "Hold it, people! You can't just leave! Wait… on second thought, you're free to go. The city thanks you!" And he saluted.

In the lobby, they headed for the elevators that would take them to the roof where the Blackbird waited. "Thank you, Emma," the Beast said drily.

"You don't think my making him salute was too much?"

"It may have been, but I kind of liked it."

The moment they were in the elevator, Cyclops said, "First order of business: When we get back up to the penthouse, someone grab one of those guns the soldiers used."

"Souvenir?" said Wolverine.

"No. I have a more practical use for it." He turned to the Beast. "What the hell were you telling me back there?'"

"I've told you about as much as I know, actually. And I got it from a reporter so inept he couldn't even get her name right, so the information is—at best—suspect. I suggest on the flight back we monitor the news radio stations and see what they're reporting. Because if it's true…"

"Good lord," said Emma.

Cyclops glanced at her. "You read my mind?"

"To save time, yes. I find it difficult to believe."

"As do I. If it's true, we have to figure out what we're going to say to the students. And I cannot emphasize this enough: We have to present a united front. Are we all agreed?"

"Yes," said Emma.

"Absolutely," said the Beast.

Wolverine nodded slightly in agreement.

Cyclops turned to Kitty, who was absentmindedly petting Lockheed. "Kitty? You agree?"

"Definitely. United front for the students. I'm on board. I just have one question."

"And that would be—?"

"What the *hell* are we talking about?"

TEN

"**...UNDER** ordinary conditions, a proposed cure for mutations would require years of testing through the Food and Drug Administration. However, according to sources, Homeland Security—which unofficially considers mutants to be an ongoing threat to national interests—has approached the Secretary of Health and Human Services to see what can be done about getting Benetech's alleged cure into circulation. As a result, a special waiver for the cure is currently being fast-tracked through channels, operating under the assumption that anyone choosing to avail themselves of the cure would be doing so of their own free will in full knowledge of any risks the cure might present. Doctor Rao, however, has insisted that the cure will not be provided to the public on a wholesale basis until she's certain that it is as safe as humanly possible..."

"Humanly possible." Kitty stared at the small television in the teachers' lounge. "Anyone else find that word choice funny?"

"Hilarious," said Logan. He didn't look amused. He wasn't.

The news then replayed excerpts from Kavita Rao's earlier conference:

"Mutants are not the next step in evolution. They are not the Homo sapiens to our Neanderthals, no matter how many times the term 'Homo superior' might be invoked by certain mutant activists. They are not the end of humankind. The mutant gene is nothing more than a disease. A corruption of healthy cellular activity. And now…at last… we have found a cure."

Logan's claws snapped out.

"Shut it off, Logan, if you'd be so kind, but preferably without slashing it to death," said Emma. She was looking distinctly uncomfortable, her fingers to the bridge of her nose, her eyes closed.

Logan picked up the remote and did as she asked. His claws remained out. The silence filled the room as if it were a living thing.

Scott, Logan, and Kitty then looked at each other. Hank was staring out the window, his back to them. Emma was looking at no one. None of them could seem to find the words to say.

But they all knew. It didn't have to be spoken.

Scott's ambitions for the positive perception of

mutants had just been kneecapped. Here they'd gone in, risked their lives—standard operating procedure, admittedly—to try to make a name for themselves as heroes and humanitarians. And now some woman, with just a few words, had demoted them from heroes to victims. Sufferers of a sickness, but hey, no worries. She held the cure in her hand and could make all the mutants just go away. No one would have to look at them or worry about them anymore. Even those horrible X-Men would be nice and safe and normal, rather than a potential threat.

"I was downstairs," Kitty said finally, breaking the silence. "Half the kids are glued to the TV in the den. The rest of them are talking about this, arguing about it. Frankly, they're freaking out. They're terrified, confused. Some of them are ecstatic, and others hate the ones who are ecstatic. They don't know how to deal with this."

"And they're giving me a sodding migraine," Emma finally spoke up. "The psychic tension is unbearable."

"Okay," said Scott. "There have been too many times in this world where the public panics because wrong information gets out. Then by the time the truth emerges, everyone's wasted a lot of time and energy getting worked up about it. For nothing. We are not going to fall into that trap. The first thing we have to find out is whether this is some kind of hoax.

Find out who this woman—"

"Kavita Rao," Hank said, so softly that Scott, Emma, and Kitty nearly didn't hear him. (Wolverine, of course, did.) "She's one of the greatest geneticists alive, and not prone to pranks." He kept his back to them. "I don't know much about this corporation, 'Benetech.' But if Doctor Rao says she can reverse mutation, there's a very good chance she can."

Emma slowly opened her eyes. The cobalt blue of her irises glittered mercilessly. "Then I guess I'll have to kill her."

"Well, *there's* a thoughtful plan," said Kitty.

"And I say 'amen' to it."

Kitty looked at Logan, who had just endorsed the concept of premeditated murder, and there was shock and even fleeting betrayal in her eyes. "Are you kidding?"

"Do I look like I'm kidding? Do I look like somebody who has a problem with killing?"

"No. I've seen you kill. But always in self-defense…"

"That's what this is. I piled up a lot of enemies in my time, kid. If I didn't have my powers, don't think for a minute they wouldn't come after me." He studied his claws clinically. "Just imagine me not having a healing factor. I'd be standing there, or more likely lying there, in agony, while blood flowed out of my hand through the gaping wounds from my claws.

Yeah. I'd be real useful."

"Logan," Kitty said worriedly, "could you...put them away, maybe? I don't know why, but they're making me a little nervous."

"I can't," he said. His tone was devoid of emotion. "The woman called me a disease. You know how that feels to me? I can't even sheathe. My claws won't go back. She said...we were...a *disease.*"

"She said the mutant *strain* was a disease," she reminded him.

"You think this Doctor Rao knows the difference? And even if she does, you think anyone else will?"

"You think the government will?" said Emma. "You heard them. They're willing to throw all caution aside to get this drug out there quickly. You think they're hurrying it along because they're anxious to give people a *choice* on the matter? If this mutant 'cure' does exist, then they will get a hold of it, and they will line us up. Those who refuse to take it voluntarily, well...they'll be attended to. Perhaps the next time we go out to fight on behalf of humanity, to show them what heroes we are, there'll be sharpshooters in place firing darts at us filled with the cure. They'll let us attend to the menace, and then they'll attend to us. Don't you see where this is heading?"

"Yeah, to murder," said Kitty. "The professor would be so proud."

Emma approached her until they were inches from each other. Kitty didn't flinch. Emma's normally reserved voice was filled with barely restrained anger and contempt. "As usual, your naïveté is neither cute nor useful. Have it your way: The government, despite all likelihood to the contrary, decides not to force the cure upon us. How secure do you expect the supply of it to be? This isn't plutonium we're talking about. It will get out. What if it falls into the hands of anti-mutant extremists?"

"Or our new buddy from another world," said Logan.

"Ord," said Scott, who had remained silent for much of the discussion. "We need to know about this guy. He drew us out for a reason."

"Yeah, right before the nice doctor lady went public," Logan pointed out. "We thinkin' that's a coincidence?"

"I don't know," said Scott. "I don't know what to…" He paused, and then looked away from the others as if he couldn't meet their gaze. He seemed…

…ashamed.

"The professor would have been ready for this," he said softly.

It was a considerable turnaround from mere hours ago, when he had led them out on their mission, speaking in confident tones of what they were going to accomplish. Now he looked isolated, alone, even though he was surrounded by friends.

"No one could have been ready for—" Kitty began.

Emma cut her off, not even bothering to look at her. "You're tired, Scott. And tomorrow is likely to be unpleasant. Why don't you get some rest? In fact," and she took in the rest of them with her gaze, "all you fine men should try to relax. That means claws in, Logan. Kitty and I will figure out how to keep the students together tonight."

"Thanks, Emma," said Scott. He sounded a bit like a lost child.

In a vain attempt to bring some levity to the somber moment, Hank suggested, "Maybe Scott and Logan could fight on the lawn again. The kids loved that."

Logan didn't rise to the bait. Instead, sheathing his claws with visible effort, he said, "I ain't up to anything don't have the word 'beer' in it."

"You could fight for beers," said Hank.

"Well, now that doesn't sound too bad."

The door closed behind them. Emma and Kitty were alone.

———————— 🪐 ————————

Well, this is cozy.

The icicle—way better name for her than White Queen—stands there like a statue, except colder and with less personality, and looks at me like the bug she obviously thinks I am.

"I'll be brief," she says. "Things are about to get very ugly for us here, so I wanted to—"

"I'm sorry, there's a part that's not already ugly?" My voice hardens. I've always been happy with a power that's mostly defensive, but right now I'd be thrilled to have eye beams or something, just so I could slap her around a little. "Scott Summers has been a leader all his life. Now I see him questioning himself, taking orders from you..."

She actually looks a little defensive. Good. Keep her off balance. "I never give—"

I don't let her have a chance; I steamroll over her. "You talk about murder, and he doesn't say a word. How do I know you're not turning him into your own private sock puppet, mentally controlling every word out of his mouth? Which, in fact, you probably are. Why doesn't anybody see...?"

"Do you know why you're here, Miss Pryde? Because I asked that you come."

"Yeah, I know that. I got your letter, remember? Because you're such a control freak that even when Scott wanted me here, you had to be the one to write to—"

"You're not following. Scott didn't want you here. He wasn't *opposed* to the idea, you understand. When I suggested it, he embraced it. But I'm the one who wanted it."

She's lying. Has to be. No way this stone-cold floozy thought I'd be a good fit here. I wonder if she knows what I'm thinking. I wonder if she'd care.

"I am in love with Scott Summers," she goes on. "And I'm very grateful to Professor Xavier for his trust. Being an X-Man means a lot to me. But it doesn't always agree with me." She's walking across the room, keeping her back to me. Keeping her eyes away from me. Is it because she thinks that, if I look into them, I'll be able to tell that she's lying? Or is it because she's vulnerable and doesn't want to be seen that way?

As if she hears what I'm thinking—which she very well might—she turns and looks me straight in the eyes. It's like she's daring me to take my best shot at discerning the real Emma Frost. "I don't have a family famous for moral fiber. I like to think I've…" She pauses, maybe aware of the irony of the word. "…evolved. But I wanted someone on the team that I hadn't really fought alongside. Someone who would watch me if I…"

Her voice trails off. She doesn't finish the sentence. She doesn't have to. I can complete it in any number of ways: Slipped. Betrayed us. Turned evil. Let the evil that was already there out.

So that's what I am? Her watchdog?

Lockheed lies nestled on the couch. He stirs, raises his head, his pupilless eyes focusing on me as if he can sense the cold, barely contained rage within me.

"The first day I ever met you," I say, "you told me you were sure we'd be great friends. A few hours later…the first time I ever met the X-Men…the first day…they were ambushed. And captured. And caged. By you. I learned more about good and evil in that one day than I ever have before or since. I was thirteen. And a half." She isn't looking at me now. She's staring straight ahead. I'm walking around her, out of her sight line, and she just keeps looking at where I was. That's appropriate. In a way, I'm looking where I was, too, or at least where I used to be—as a person, as an X-Man—and thinking about how her actions shaped me into that. "When I think about evil...whenever I think about the concept of evil, yours is the face I see. I don't have to watch you, Miss Frost. I can smell you."

I toss one last look her way and phase through the wall. It's the best I can come up with for a dramatic exit. Lockheed, watching me leave, seems to shrug and go back to sleep. He can keep an eye on her. If she gives him any difficulties, I'm sure he'll have no problem ripping her head off and eating it.

I just hope he doesn't get food poisoning.

ELEVEN

THE security guards outside Benetech had had a busy evening. It had seemed as if every news media outlet in the world was present at the press conference, but apparently a metric ton of them hadn't shown up, and now they were endeavoring to make up for lost time. But the guards were under strict instructions to let no one past the large, gated entrance, and they took their jobs very seriously. So all afternoon, well into the evening, they'd stood there with their rifles in evidence, watching an array of TV reporters do their stand-ups in front of the facility. The reporters had approached the subject matter in different ways, but all ultimately came to the same conclusion: The mutant menace was nearly at an end.

Doctor Rao had not emerged. She practically lived at the place, but usually by this point she would have finally gone home. Not tonight. It was easy to figure out why. Reporters had probably found out where she lived and were camped out, waiting for her to show. Smart lady, the guards believed, to keep a low profile. Then again, the fact that she was a smart lady was what had gotten her into this situation in the first place.

Since she wasn't coming out, and no one else was attempting to get in, it looked to be another quiet night. But the guards remained vigilant. They kept a wary eye on the entrance, silently daring anyone to approach them and try to get inside. There was no way they were going to allow that.

As it happened, none of them were looking up. If they had, they would have seen a dark, furred figure with a large yellow "X" festooned across its costume, leaping over their heads, highlighted against a full moon. They continued to stand guard, convinced they were doing their job and unaware that they had, in fact, failed spectacularly.

THE Beast scaled the wall effortlessly. Benetech might have fancied itself a highly secure facility, but they had never prepared themselves for someone like him. *Perhaps I could pick up some extra cash this way. Secure facilities can hire me to try to break in to determine just how airtight their security is.* He considered it briefly, but then dismissed it. One never knew when a place just like this could wind up posing a threat, and he far preferred to be able to gain access at will.

He'd already managed to hack into the facility's system and determine the location of Doctor Rao's lab. His photographic memory kept the map securely in his head. Now it was just a matter of reaching the lab so that he could start looking around. It was late enough that he was certain he would be able to work undetected.

He made it to the roof and crossed it stealthily. There was no door, but there was a cat burglar's best friend: a skylight. It was triple-ply thick, securely latched and alarmed.

Beast wondered why the skylight was there in the first place, but he thought: *Don't knock it.* It was his way in.

He could have punched through it, but that would have triggered the wiring and sounded the alarm. Instead he pulled out a handy little instrument from the small knapsack he had slung over his shoulder. He secured the gadget's suction cup against the glass and activated it. A tiny laser, secured to the suction cup by a small rod, flared to life and began to slice into the window. He eased the laser around; the result was a perfect circle, which he was then able to extract with no problem.

He could see the small box on the edge of the window's inside that provided the connection to the alarm system. "Child's play," he muttered, extracting a screwdriver from the knapsack. He eased his arm through, holding the screwdriver, and managed to disconnect it from the rest of the system in less than a minute. Moments later he unlatched the skylight and eased himself through.

A large, dark room opened up beneath him. It was filled with intersecting red beams, which—were they broken by something such as, say, a blue-furred body—would sound any number of alarms.

"Hunh. That's new," Beast muttered.

He studied the array for a full minute, mentally charted a trajectory, and then launched himself into the air. He twisted and turned in midair as he fell, finding the gaps in the crossbeams, taking advantage of them. He landed silently on the floor in a crouch, realizing only belatedly that if the floor was pressure-sensitive, he was in trouble. But there was nothing, or at least nothing he could hear or detect.

He exited the room. There might have been important and useful things in there, but he had no interest in them. He was focused with precision, as laser-like as the beams he had just eluded.

Moving through the empty corridors, sticking to the shadows, he made it to Doctor Rao's lab. There was a security keypad outside, but he'd prepared for that as well. He extracted a blank security card attached to an electronic reader and slid it into the slot in the keypad. Seconds later the code numbers appeared on its screen and he tapped them into the pad. The keypad beeped at him welcomingly, and the door slid open.

Beast clambered upward, preferring to make his way across the ceiling in the darkened lab. His night vision was perfect. Even upside down, he was positive he'd be able to find what he was looking for. The only sound in the place was the soft clicking of his claws against the ceiling.

And then another click. The sound of a light switch, which was all the warning he had before the room was flooded with illumination. He squinted against it, his eyes hurting from the abrupt change.

"Doctor McCoy," came a soft, accented, slightly mocking female voice.

He looked down. She was standing there calmly, looking up at him.

"Doctor Rao," he replied. He dropped from the ceiling and landed on the floor. "It's been a long time. Berlin, wasn't it? The cloning seminar…?" He was endeavoring to sound casual. He knew perfectly well the last time they'd seen each other, and that she was aware of it as well.

"I seem to recall you were far less…furry…back then. Much more—"

"Human?" He shrugged. "Appearances can be deceiving, can't they."

"Yes, they can," she said. "If I may ask: what happened?"

"An unfortunate experiment that tried to make me something other than what I was…and instead brought out my true nature. As I said, appearances…"

"Can be deceiving, yes. For instance, there are armed guards waiting outside the door, packing enough gas guns to put Galactus to sleep. Did you really think you could break in here?"

He was slightly annoyed by that, realizing there must have indeed been pressure alarms built into the floor. Apparently he'd been monitored all along. But he maintained an air of bravado. "Did you think I wouldn't try?" He approached her, remaining in a defensive crouch. "You've thrown a bomb into the room, Doctor. People will die because of what you've done today."

"People will die? How can someone with the eyes of a cat be so blind? People *have* died. People *are* dying. You say people will die? I say innocent people will live. Will live decent, normal lives."

Beast was now standing upright. "Yes, I saw you trundling out your poster child. Nice piece of publicity Tildie's buying you. Well played."

"I'm not playing, Doctor McCoy. There are people whose lives have been destroyed by unwanted mutation, and I will give my life to help them. Whatever you and your X-Men plan to do, I—"

Then she stopped and, to the Beast's surprise, laughed softly.

"Do you find that funny?" he asked.

She didn't answer immediately. When she did, she said, "During our time in Berlin, did I ever tell you about Harish?"

"Harish? No, the name doesn't ring a bell."

"He was my best friend when I was a child in India, in a small village you've never heard of. The sweetest boy. He was an artist. He was always sketching, always drawing. Still lifes. People. Me."

"Are we about to get to the part where you posed naked for him wearing only the Heart of the Ocean? Because if so—"

"And then one morning," she continued as if he hadn't spoken, "shortly after he'd turned fourteen, his parents ran screaming from their small house, which was barely more than four metal walls held together through sheer willpower. Their son, they screamed, had turned into a monster. Overnight he had developed horns and a green hue to his face. Can you guess what happened next?"

He didn't have to. She told him anyway.

"They dragged him out into the street, which was little more than a dirt road, and declared that a demon had wandered into our midst. And in their fear and terror, they beat him, Doctor McCoy. They beat him to death in front of my eyes, and I stood there and did nothing because there were so many of them and I was just one girl. But there was more to it than that. I was afraid that if I acted on his behalf, they'd turn on me as well. So I stood there, a prisoner of my helplessness and cowardice, and Harish was soon nothing but a bloodied pulp on the ground. Even his parents joined in. Even his parents. He…"

Her eyes misted a moment, and then she reached deeply into herself to find the words she needed. "Never again. Never again am I going to do nothing to help poor, tortured people like Harish when I have the ability to—"

"Kavita," he said, dropping the honorific, his voice soft. "Stop." She did so. "I'm not here to discuss the ethics of your 'mutant cure.' And I'm not here to destroy it. I just…want to know if it works."

She regarded him with open curiosity. "I…was not expecting you to say that, honestly. But in retrospect, I suppose I should not be surprised. All things considered…"

"All things, yes." He nodded toward the door. "There aren't really men with guns standing outside, are there? I'd have heard them."

"No, there aren't. I was bluffing. How'd I do?"

"You were brilliant. I was completely taken in."

"No, you weren't. Wait here, please."

He did as she requested. She disappeared into an

adjoining room that he could only assume was another lab. It was entirely possible that she was genuinely summoning security, but for some reason he had a feeling she wasn't going to do that. Then again, he'd been wrong before. He hoped this would not be one of those instances.

A long minute passed, and then Kavita Rao reemerged. She was holding a small metal box. She walked up to the Beast and opened it so he could see the contents. It was a test tube, filled with a milky liquid, nestled in a cushion of foam rubber.

"Do what you want with it," she said. She closed the box and flipped shut a small latch.

"What's the catch?"

"There's no catch. I know you, Henry. You tend to get what you want. It either happens now, simply, without anyone getting hurt. Or it happens later after a lot of people get hurt, mostly Benetech employees just trying to do their jobs. I'd rather just cut to the chase, as it were."

She handed it to him. For just a moment her finger brushed against his. A small jolt seemed to jump between them, and then he took the sample of the cure securely in his large hands. "Thank you," he said.

"Not a problem. I assume I can count on your discretion? It's only a single sample, but Benetech considers it proprietary material."

"If you're asking whether I'd turn around and give it to another think tank and let them horn in on your discovery, don't concern yourself. The last thing I want to do is facilitate people making more of it."

"Then that's that. I assume you can see yourself out."

"Absolutely."

She turned and walked away from him, and then stopped. Her shoulders squared, she said quietly, "There's been no one since you, Henry. No one even came close."

And then she walked out the door.

"YOU *did what? Are you insane?"*

Tildie was sleeping soundly. A simple enough activity for normal people, which Tildie now blessedly was.

A far more abnormal individual loomed over her, filled with fury, watching her from inside the observation room that oversaw the entirety of her world. His head was visibly scarred from being lit on fire by a dragon, and his right eye was swollen shut.

"The casual observer," said Kavita Rao calmly, "would perhaps not consider me the unbalanced one."

"You gave the X-Men the serum."

"I gave an old colleague a sample."

"Where is he?" Ord snarled. "I want to have a consult with him."

"Long gone. Do you think I'd mention it to you if there were the slightest chance you could turn this into an excuse for a brawl? Besides," and she shrugged, "they were bound to get hold of it sooner or later."

Ord didn't seem impressed by her logic. "You know what the X-Men are to me."

"Besides an excuse to go around behaving like a super villain? I saw your 'diversion' on the news. Mercenaries. Hired thugs in a room full of innocent people. It's inexcusable."

"You," said Ord, stabbing a finger at her, "should show respect, Earthspawn. Without my technologies, you would have no cure."

"The technologies are of your *people*. Your own contributions have been a great deal more… ambiguous."

"My 'contribution' is yet to come. In the meantime, the mutants will pay for what they did to my face."

Yes, because you were such a hot commodity on date nights before that happened. "The dragon did it to your face," she corrected him. "The dragon isn't a mutant. He's an alien, like you. Try to get it straight." Ord glowered at her with his one visible eye. "Your anger is a liability. You should keep it in check."

Then an armored hand clamped down on her shoulder, jolting her. "One day, Doctor Rao, you will see my anger."

She fought a wave of nausea that threatened to incapacitate her. His touch was vile. Part of her wanted to scream for Henry to return and stop this creature from ever laying a hand on her again. But she'd been speaking the truth when she'd said Henry was long gone.

She pulled her shoulder away from Ord. He could have held on to it, but instead he released it, apparently feeling he'd proven his point. "You are a pawn, my esteemed Doctor Rao," he said, "in a grand scheme. You could not comprehend its scope."

"Then I won't try," she said carelessly. She walked over to the observation window and looked down upon Tildie, sleeping, devoid of nightmares. "I have more important concerns."

TWELVE

———————— 🖋 ————————

EDWARD Tancredi didn't know he was going to punch Jay Guthrie in the face until he did it.

Jay was in the den, watching the *News at Noon.* Of course, the news people were talking about the cure.

Jay was a fairly quiet individual, the same as Edward. He tended to keep to himself and seemed a bit uncomfortable with people. His hair was a disarrayed mass of red, and on his back he sported huge reddish-brown wings that he kept enfolded around his upper body when he was sitting. The wings, and the power of flight they provided him, prompted his code name of "Icarus." They all had code names. Edward's was "Wing," which somehow seemed more appropriate to Jay's look than his own. Indeed, Hisako had suggested that Edward change his code name to "Float," but he'd disagreed, convinced he'd be subjected to endless ice-cream jokes.

Jay glanced up at him and said, "Eddie, Eddie, Eddie Tancredi," which prompted Edward to think he might as well have gone with "Float" after all, if people were going to find something related to his name to kid him about. Jay nodded toward the TV. "Check it out."

Edward walked in and saw, on the screen, footage of a long line of mutants standing outside the Benetech labs. Crowd-control barricades had been set up, forming the mutants into lines, the most massive lines Edward had seen since the last time he'd attended the San Diego Comic-Con. Some of the mutants looked relatively "normal." The others had their mutations on the outside, an array of people with scaled skin, a walrus face, bodies of various colors. A rainbow coalition.

The newscaster was saying, "Hundreds of alleged mutants are lined up outside the Benetech labs demanding this 'cure,' with more showing up every hour. A Benetech spokesman says that with the proposal to expedite the FDA approvals stalled in committee due to opposition from the formidable Senator Kelly, it will be weeks before they can even begin a federal approval process for the serum…"

Edward watched the way Jay was staring at the television. He saw a longing in Jay's face that made his gut twist in disgust. He picked up the remote and shut it off, causing Jay to snap his head around and look at him in irritation. "Dude, what the hell...?"

"You're going to do it, aren't you?"

"I haven't even thought about it..."

"Yeah, you have. I can tell."

"What are you, psychic now, too?" Jay got up from the chair and started to walk out, but Edward stepped in front of him. "Come on, dude, move..."

"Be honest," said Edward challengingly.

Jay was about to brush him aside again, but then he stopped and looked defiantly at the shorter Edward. "Okay, fine. I've been thinking about it. Okay? I've been thinking about nothing but."

"And you'd give up this?" Edward began to float, the simplest manifestation of his abilities. "You'd give up this...all this..."

"No, but maybe I'd give up all this," and he extended his wings, knocking over an empty bottle of soda. "You think this is what I wanted from my life? I had it all planned, man. I was gonna be in a band. I wanted singing to be my life. When I begged my mother to get me guitar lessons at age six—when I was practicing until my fingers bled—do you really think I was planning to sprout wings and have my life go completely off track?"

"It didn't go off track! This *is* the track, and you're having the ride of your life."

"Says you! The way it is now, the only way I get to be a famous singer is in some alternate universe where there's no more mutants. Instead I'm stuck in this one, and it sucks! I'll probably wind up dead before I'm twenty!"

"I just…" Edward shook his head. "I can't believe you're going to turn into one of those lemmings, sending the wrong message…"

"What's the 'wrong message?' What the hell are you talking ab—"

"That it's okay! That it's okay to just…just stick a needle in someone's arm and make them into something they're not! *This* is what you are!" and he grabbed one of Jay's wings.

Jay reflexively yanked it clear. He thumped his chest and said, "No! This is what I am! In here! But when people look at me they just see a bunch of feathers on my back!" His voice rose in anger. "And if I decide I want to get rid of them, then that's my choice! Okay, you little jerk?" He tried to move past him, and Edward's fist flew as if by its own accord. He hit Jay squarely in the face, splitting his lip. Jay put his hand to his mouth, and it came away with blood.

He lunged at Edward and missed clean as Edward vaulted straight up, out of reach. But then Jay opened his mouth, filling the room with high-powered sonics. Edward clapped his hands to his ears, his focus gone, and the moment he was on the ground, Jay was upon him. He slammed Edward to the floor and tried to punch him in the face. Edward raised his forearms to absorb the blows.

The sounds of battle were bringing other students running, and Edward was seized with a desperation to get out from under the pounding he was taking from Jay. That desperation translated into fury. He grabbed the bottle that had fallen off the table by the neck and brought it up and around, banging it into the side of Jay's head. Edward didn't have much upper-body strength, so it was hardly a lethal blow, but it was sufficient to dislodge him. He tumbled back. Edward scrambled to his feet and hauled Jay up with one hand, which was easy to do since Jay's bones were fairly light.

Had he been thinking ahead—had he indeed had any serious combat training—Edward would have realized the flaw in that tactic. If he'd kept Jay on his back, Jay's wings would have been pinned and useless. As it was, because he was upright, Jay's wings were freed. They began to flap with great ferocity, propelling the two of them toward a picture window. Just as other students arrived on the scene, Edward and Jay smashed through the window.

On television and in the movies, people crashed through windows and quickly bounded to their feet, surrounded by broken glass but ready for more fighting. The reality, Edward learned, was very different.

He and Jay lay dazed on the ground, outside the building. Jay's wings had actually absorbed much of the impact, but it was still enough to rattle both their brains. And the glass was sharp. Both of them had cuts and gashes on their faces and upper arms, and rips in their shirts.

They lay there amid the shattered glass, gasping for air. It was an effort for both of them to stand. The world swirled around Edward as he tried to focus. Through lips that were already swelling up, he said thickly, "You…are *such* a *tool*…"

Even though the world was still spinning from his point of view, Edward began to rise off the ground. "Come up here and say that."

"You got it." Jay's wings started to flap. Edward immediately covered his eyes as little bits of glass flew in all directions. Jay backed up, shaking the last of the glass from his feathers. Then he suddenly angled downward, dive-bombing toward Edward.

They were still only a couple feet off the ground, and Edward started to rise to meet the charge. Abruptly something grabbed him around the ankle and yanked hard. He was helpless to resist as he was slammed to the ground with even more force than when he'd crashed through the window.

Logan looked down at Edward with great annoyance.

Jay tried to brake, but he had too much speed going downward. Without even deigning to look in his direction, Logan swung his palm back, catching Jay across the face. Had Logan made the move at full speed, it would have crushed Jay's skull. As it was, the strength of the Adamantium skeleton inside Logan's hand was sufficient to knock Jay to one side. Spiraling at an angle, he ricocheted off the side of the building and rolled to a stop two feet away from Edward.

There was silence for a moment. Then Logan said in obvious disgust, "I'd ask what this was all about if I gave a crap. You're both idiots."

Jay hung his head, but Edward still had enough spirit in him to say, "Right, because getting into fights...you'd never do anything like that."

Logan reached down and picked up one of the largest shards of glass. Without a word he slid it across his forearm, leaving a vicious trail of blood. He held the arm up to Edward's face. Edward felt a little sick, seeing such a nasty gash so close up.

Within seconds it had healed over completely. There wasn't the slightest hint of any damage.

"Can you do that?" said Logan. Edward shook his head. "Then shut up."

"Yessir," said Edward.

"Get your asses to the infirmary..."

"No need." One of the other students, Josh Foley, was climbing out the window. His skin was golden;

even his tousled hair shared the same color. If he'd been bald, he'd have looked like an Oscar statue come to life. He dropped to the ground and walked quickly over to them. He put one hand on Edward's arm and another on Jay's.

It took Josh a full minute to cause the gashes in their skin and all other damage to melt away, just as Wolverine's injuries had vanished.

"Handy," said Logan. "What do they call you again?"

"Elixir," Josh said. He sounded a bit dubious. "I'm not wild about it. I was hoping for something like," and he held up a hand and said dramatically, "Messiah." Then he paused when he saw Logan's face. "Too much?"

"Just a little." Logan turned to Jay and chucked a thumb toward the mansion. "You, in there. You, the wingless wonder: over there. Stay there until someone comes for you." He pointed toward a bench situated some distance away in the garden. "I don't want the two of you in the same place until you've had a chance to cool off. Understood?"

"Yessir," Edward said once more.

He rose up off the ground and took one last defiant look at Jay. "This is who we are," he said, and then glided across the way to the bench.

He was still sitting there when Kitty Pryde plopped down onto the seat next to him. He glanced at her. She smiled. He didn't smile back.

"So I understand we had a problem a bit earlier," said Kitty.

He shrugged.

"Ah, the teenage shrug," she said. "I know it well. Done it myself more than once."

"You say that like you're so much older than me," retorted Edward. "You're not, y'know. Only a few years."

"It's not the years, honey. It's the mileage." When he didn't reply, she said, *"Raiders of the Lost Ark."*

"I know. I get it."

"Good. But I don't get why you're suddenly throwing down with Icarus. You want to fill me in on that?"

He didn't answer immediately. He stared off into the sky, imagining himself there, his arms spread wide, the wind in his face, the feeling of complete and utter freedom. It was incomparable. Who in their right mind would even think of giving that up, of becoming less than they were?

He continued the stream of consciousness into actual words, not caring that he wasn't directly answering Kitty's question. "First time I landed, I broke both my legs."

She nodded, not interrupting him.

"I kinda just assumed if I was flying, I was invulnerable, too. Which is, uhm...not actually that bright," he admitted sheepishly. "But you know...

they sometimes go together and yeah, then I was freaked out for a while, just freaked by the whole concept. It was *unnatural.* But when I got good at it... when I *got* it, I mean...

"*Flying.* Jeez...

"When you're flying, the world goes away. It makes everything else...smaller...and sort of okay, too. It's the most important feeling. I can't lose that."

"So that's what this is about? You think you're going to be forced to give up your power?"

"Among other things."

"Okay, well that's just not gonna happen."

He looked at her as if noticing her for the first time. "It's not?"

"Wing," she said patiently, "just 'cause someone goes on TV and says they have a 'cure for mutation,' that doesn't mean it's true. And even if it is...nobody's gonna force it on you. Mutants are a community. We're a people, and there's no way anybody can make us become what *they* want. We stick together...you'll see. We're stronger than this."

He did nothing to keep the incredulity from his face or voice. "Miss Pryde...are you a freaking idiot?"

She scowled. Which wasn't that big a deal. Logan scowls, you worry he's going to gut you. Kitty Pryde scowls, and it's almost kinda cute.

"Ex-*cuse* me?" she said. "I'm not thrilled about

your tone or your word choice—"

"Miss Pryde, we got people gunning for us with a serum that castrates us, and you're worrying about my word choice? *Really?*" He shook his head, trying to find a way to get through to her, desperate to convey his concerns. "Look...I told you what it was like to fly. So there's Jay, and he must have the same feelings I do about flying. He *has* to. There's no way he couldn't. But he was willing to just toss it all away. I mean...if it's a mutant whose power is that he has red flaky skin that itches all the time, and it keeps falling off and regrowing and he's in actual, physical pain 24/7, then okay, yeah, I get it. Then it's like a cure for your own personal hell. Fine. No one in his right mind could have a problem with that. But there's Jay, and there's others too, I know it, I've heard them talking about it. I mean, I know it was a hologram, but that Sentinel crashing through...Jeez. You're training us to survive in a world where giant robots and evil mutants are going to try and kill us. How many others of us are gonna say, 'Screw that. I'm just gonna be normal, and then those things won't be out to kill us anymore.'"

"And there will still be evil mutants running around," said Kitty, "except people who embrace the cure won't be able to defend themselves or anyone else."

"Exactly," said Edward, "which means the government's gonna start rounding up the evil mutants to get rid of them. To make sure they can't do any damage. And you know what happens then? They start rounding up *all* the mutants just to make sure none of the good ones turn evil and become a threat. And at some point soon, real soon, they're just gonna decide, y'know, what the hell: good, evil, makes no difference. Just take away their powers and make the world safe for all the nice, normal humans. The humans who maim and murder and rape and become serial killers and dictators who commit genocide against their own people. Because the world's *so* much better having nice, normal people like that instead of people with powers who might be able to *stop* them.

"And that's when they'll be coming for me, Miss Pryde. That's when they'll be coming for me. Because guys like Jay are going to make everyone else think the world is divided into two types of mutants: the evil ones who need to be stopped, and all the others who wish—sometimes secretly, sometimes openly— that they could just be rid of their powers. So when the government comes around and forces it down our throats, there won't be a damned thing we can do about it.

"So instead of lecturing me about the mutant community, maybe you should be trying to figure out a way to bury this whole building underground so no one can ever find us and take our powers away." He raised his voice and demanded, "*You get it now? Do you finally freaking get it? Do you even believe one word of the crap you're trying to sell me? Huh? Do you?*

She got up and walked away without another word. Edward shouted after her, *"I guess that's my answer, huh?"* Seconds later he was alone again, left to stare at the sky, wondering when—not if—its heights would be denied him.

EMMA Frost was in the teachers' lounge, pouring coffee for herself, when Kitty Pryde stalked in, her fists clenched. Logan sat in an easy chair, his legs up, watching CNN's coverage of the cure. The ubiquitous line of massed mutants at the Benetech facility was on the screen. "Where's Scott?" demanded Kitty.

"He took the Blackbird," said Emma. "Something about an appointment. Since he wasn't in his battle gear, I assume it was merely information gathering."

Emma didn't require a telepath's ability to know Kitty was upset. Kitty's face was red, and her body trembled with barely suppressed fury. And if all that hadn't been enough of a dead giveaway, the fact that Kitty actually spoke to her like a person, even a colleague, rather than using Plan A (ignoring her) or Plan B (excoriating her), spoke volumes.

"How much detention are we allowed to give?" Kitty asked her. "What's the maximum amount of detention the human body can withstand?"

Tread carefully, Emma thought. *Don't bother pointing out our bodies aren't human. Be sympathetic. Commiserate.*

"Counseling going well, then?" Emma asked.

"Great."

"Let me guess. The *'mutants are a community'* line didn't quite fly."

Kitty made an irritated noise. "Don't talk to me about flying right now. As far as I'm concerned, everyone who can fly right now can take a flying leap."

"You looked at the news, punkin'?" said Logan. He switched the television to mute. Subtitles snapped on, detailing much of the same reportage as before. Other than the swelling ranks of mutants who would prefer to be former mutants, nothing had changed.

"Mutants aren't a community, Katherine," said Emma. "They're pathetic sheep, begging to be shorn."

"You really have a thing about comparing people to sheep, don't you," said Kitty.

Emma ignored her. She put down her coffee cup and started ticking off offenses on her fingers. "Three students were missing from my ethics class. Seventeen missing from the school, overall. While you were dealing with the aftermath of the fistfight that Logan broke up, he had to attend to a second one, *and* a mystical swordfight. And that dreadful Guatemalan crab-boy...*what* was his name...?"

"Felipe," Logan reminded her.

"Right. Felipe is at Benetech telling reporters this is every mutant's only chance to avoid burning in everlasting hellfire. This business with the cure is eating us from the inside out."

She picked up her coffee and started to sip it, then noticed Kitty staring at her with a look of amazement.

"Oh my God," Kitty said. "*You* teach *ethics?*"

That's her takeaway from this?

"Yes. *Do* let's make jokes right now," said Emma.

"I'm not joking. I have a very large problem with that concept."

Emma tossed aside all notions of trying to make nice. "Our students are fleeing the school, you half-wit!"

"Well, maybe it's time for another peppy *'They will always hate us'* speech. I'm sure *that* helped."

"I thought *I* was the one with the claws," muttered Logan.

"Are we really back to that, Katherine?" said Emma. "That's ancient history."

"It was two days ago! And that, along with your *'Here's-a-Sentinel-to-scare-the-piss-out-of-you welcome package,'* is part of the reason why Eddie is completely paranoid about the government taking away his powers."

"It's hardly paranoia if they *are* out to get you."

"Yeah, there's a new thought."

"At least it's more realistic than your

Pollyanna—"

A low, exhausted growl from the doorway stopped both of the women in midstream. Hank entered slowly, rubbing his eyes. The growl was followed by a request that, in its tone, sounded more animal than human. "Just tell me there's coffee."

Kitty immediately picked up the coffee pot. Hank, who normally moved with astounding fluidity, was shuffling as if anchors were attached to his feet. "Maybe we could just hook me up with an IV," he suggested.

"Have you been up all night?" said Emma in surprise.

Hank reached for a mug that read '*Women Love Me; Fish Fear Me*' and held it out. Kitty filled it. "I was in the lab. Checking out a sample of Doctor Rao's serum."

Emma looked stunned. "How did you—?"

"She gave it to me."

If he had walked in and announced that he was going to move to Seattle and start giving psychiatric advice on the radio, he could not have received a more astounded look from the others. Logan took his feet off the ottoman one at a time and placed them on the floor. Emma just stared at Hank. Kitty nearly let the pot slip out of her hand.

Instead of acknowledging their shock, Hank gazed into the coffee cup, assessing it. "Peruvian blond, first beans of the season," he said in an affected British accent, the one he used when he was trying to sound like James Bond. "Emma, your taste never fails to impress." He took another sip. Then, sounding like himself again, he continued, "I went to see Kavita. She agreed I should verify her results and gave me a sample. I'll be a day at most."

And with that he walked out of the teachers' lounge, leaving his colleagues in stunned silence.

"SOMEBODY'S gonna die. You know how I know this? 'Cause I'm gonna kill 'em."

Nick Fury, the head of S.H.I.E.L.D., was not one to issue threats lightly. That was something Scott knew from personal experience. Indeed, it had been Fury's famed prickly personality, and his tendency to view anyone and everyone as a potential threat, that had prompted Scott to wear his street clothes when flying the Blackbird up to the S.H.I.E.L.D. Helicarrier. Like it or not, his costume—any costume, really—could be interpreted as an invitation to a fight. He had no desire to make Fury think he had come to S.H.I.E.L.D. to start trouble.

Fury was an old military man. It was obvious in his attitude, in his bearing. There were some who claimed he'd fought as far back as World War II, which Scott didn't give much credence to. This was not a man in his eighties, nor was Fury a mutant. It wasn't like he had a healing factor. So either "Nick Fury" was a name secretly passed down from father to son, along with the eyepatch, or else the rumors about him were greatly exaggerated.

Still, however long Fury had been around, there was no question that he was a soldier through and through. And as a soldier, Fury saw the entire world as a potential war zone, and everyone in it as a possible enemy. Best to provide him as little reason to be suspicious as possible.

Fury was cradling the sleek machine gun that Scott had salvaged from the penthouse. His one eye studied it, his hands hefting the weapon. He was not a happy spy.

"So it *is* one of yours," said Scott.

Fury nodded curtly. "The casing's been modified, but the package is definitely S.H.I.E.L.D. design. Experimental. Very new."

They stood on the landing bay of the Helicarrier, near a desk where the deck officer typically sat. The Helicarrier was aptly named: The main deck looked very much like a typical aircraft carrier, with various air vehicles routinely landing upon it and taking off from it. But it was kept aloft some thirty thousand feet courtesy of four gigantic engines, two forward and two aft. The airborne vehicle enabled S.H.I.E.L.D. to go anywhere in the world within hours, and that had proven an extremely valuable asset any number of times in the past.

Upon Scott's arrival, Fury had appeared immediately and told the deck officer to take five. It was clear that Fury intended to meet with Scott right there. On the one hand Scott understood this, since it was the most efficient means of dealing with the matter at hand. On the other hand, the X-Men leader realized Fury wasn't the least bit interested in allowing him access to the floating facility beyond his point of entrance. Scott tried not to feel insulted by that.

Fury was disassembling the gun on the desk, inspecting the components. "If one of those clowns had gotten a round off near civilians once it went hot…"

"We made sure they didn't," said Scott. He'd thought as much: that firing bullets was just one of the gun's capabilities. Seeing the gun in parts, he noted what looked like a grenade launcher, a flame thrower, a pulse blaster, and several other offensive options that he didn't even recognize. Once it really got revved up, genuinely locked and loaded, a single one of the weapons might well have been able to annihilate the entire penthouse. Scott couldn't help but wonder if Ord knew what the firearms were really capable of. And if Ord had known, would he even care?

"What are a bunch of second-rate mercs doing with S.H.I.E.L.D. weaponry that isn't even in the field yet?"

"If I knew that, I'd be killing somebody already," said Fury, taking a seat behind the desk.

"Yes, so you said. So the next question is, what are a bunch of second-rate mercs doing with a psychotic alien warrior? 'Ord of the Breakworld.' Any bells?"

"Breakworld is what we call the room with the coffee maker and snack machines, but I doubt there's any connection. You know for sure this guy's an ET?" said Fury.

"Well, we were in the middle of a firefight, so we didn't really have a chance to hook him up to a polygraph. In terms of absolute proof, right now I don't know too much."

"So he could be anything."

Scott didn't love where this was going.

Sure enough, Fury pointed out, "Could even be a mutant."

Scott's lips suddenly felt very dry. He leaned forward on the desk. "Am I missing something?"

"I just don't have a lot to go on, is all."

"You know about this 'cure' thing, right? 'Mutants are a disease'? This monster shows up right when all that comes out, running a crew carrying *your* ordnance, and the best you can do is accuse him of being one of *us?*"

He hadn't intended to sound so challenging, but he couldn't help himself. Ord had nearly killed them, and Fury was insinuating that—what? That the X-Men had brought it on themselves somehow?

Fury's face tightened, his single eye staring daggers at Scott. "Don't get in my face, boy. That ain't a right you've earned." He paused to let that sink in, and then said, "I let you up here 'cause Xavier's got some cred with the powers and he says you're in charge. Now I'll run this name down, this 'Ord,' and I'll share whatever I find." Then he got to his feet, bringing himself up to eye level. "But if he's got some beef with your team, that problem's not mine. And if you think anybody here is losing sleep over whether you mutants might all suddenly lose your powers, well…then you ain't been to Manhattan lately."

"Yes, we have, actually, and that gun in front of you serves as proof. We went there to save lives. You can hover around in this vehicle like the god of espionage all you want. But we mere mortals were down there, getting our hands dirty to save a bunch of people who, God willing, *won't* automatically be assuming that we're exactly the same as the creature we saved them from. We can do a lot of good, and if we had people like you trusting us and working with us, instead of trying to figure out how everything that goes wrong is somehow our fault, then we could do even more good."

"Trust you."

"That's right."

"Trust a group that's been known to give aid and comfort to enemies. Like your boy, Magneto."

"What exactly makes him our boy?" said Scott.

"He taught at your damn school."

"Back when he was a *lot* more stable. What makes you think we would knowingly harbor a dangerous criminal?"

"How's Miss Frost?" said Fury.

Scott was taken aback.

Fury pressed the point. "We're watching very close. That's our job. Any further threat from your camp, we're gonna know about it ahead of time."

With cold, quiet anger, Scott said, "Duly noted. Should we be providing you the same service regarding the Black Widow? Former Russian spy. Now she works for you. Just in case you're not staying on top of that, we can help out. Thirty seconds with 'Miss Frost,' and we can tell you whether you have a double agent in your midst. Because cleaning up after the messes that humans make is *our* job. And if you can't see that, well, then even for a guy with one eye, your vision's incredibly narrow."

Fury glared at him. Scott suddenly started measuring relative speeds in his head, wondering if he could snap open his visor and fire before Fury pulled out his gun and put a bullet in Scott's brain. He hoped it wouldn't come to that. This was Nick Fury. He could just gun down Scott Summers and make up the excuse later. Hell, by the time Emma and the others realized he was overdue, Fury could have weighted down Scott's body and dumped it into the Marianas Trench, and disassembled the Blackbird into spare parts.

And then, his voice flat and even, Fury said, "I hear about this 'Ord,' I'll give you a call. You know the way out."

Inwardly, Scott let out a sigh of relief. He knew he'd pushed it about as far as he could with Fury. He'd said enough to make it clear the X-Men were not to be trifled with, but not so much that his photograph wound up on the side of a milk carton. He gave a slight nod, which Fury silently acknowledged.

Minutes later Scott was in the Blackbird, angling down and away from the Helicarrier. He continued to marvel at the massive airship's size. He also realized he was bracing himself, anticipating that Fury might open fire on him and blow him to bits. Scott didn't fully relax until he was a safe distance from the Helicarrier.

Then again, this *was* S.H.I.E.L.D. he was talking about. Their reach extended pretty damned far, and he wasn't sure it was truly possible to escape.

* * * *

FURY remained where he was until the Blackbird was long gone.

He didn't have to turn around to know that someone was standing behind him. Fury was always hyperaware of his surroundings, including this woman who seemed to prefer shadows to light.

"You can come out. He's gone now," Fury said.

She did as he instructed. Light glinted off her black sunglasses, and her long green hair was tied back into a ponytail. The sharp red of her lipstick stood out starkly against the faint pallor of her skin.

"What do you think he knows?" she said.

"He told us himself. Right now he doesn't know much. He's got guesses, suspicions. That's about it."

"I suppose it doesn't matter. Even if he knew everything…who would he get to listen? Where would he go for help? If it came down to his word against ours, who would believe him?"

"You're underestimating him, Brand. If 'it' came down to anything, he wouldn't be looking anywhere for help other than to his teammates. Make no mistake, we can take them if we have to. But it ain't gonna be fun, and it's gonna end bloody. And that's to no one's advantage, including ours."

"How would taking the X-Men out of the picture not be to our advantage?"

"Because," said Fury, "some day, we might find ourselves in crap up to our eyes and sayin' to ourselves, 'Gee…might be nice to have a guy with force-beam eyeballs or a lunatic with claws in his hands helping us out. Oh, right…they ain't available because we had to take 'em out.'"

He turned to face her. It was an unusual stare-down, two people with only one visible eye between them. "And if this situation you dumped in our laps causes that to happen, well…I ain't gonna be pleased. We on the same page, Brand?"

"Yes, sir."

"Good. Don't forget it."

"No chance of that, sir."

Her voice was flat, inflectionless, like a machine's. *No. Not a machine's,* thought Fury. *I've known machines that have way more compassion than Abigail Brand.*

Brand said nothing as Fury walked away. Her thoughts were her own. They always were.

THIRTEEN

IF Hank hadn't been quite so wrapped up in his analysis of the sample, he would have realized much earlier that he was in trouble.

When Logan entered Hank's lab, he did so with a very light footfall. As preoccupied as Hank was, he was still able to perceive Logan's arrival. He did not, however, connect the dots and realize that Logan was in hunting mode, nor ponder just who or what Logan might be stalking.

"How's it going?" Logan asked casually.

"Fine." Hank had his eye glued to a microscope. He was busy watching a drop of the serum interact with a drop of mutant blood, specifically his own.

"Got an answer yet? Been a few hours."

"It's not conclusive."

Logan let the answer hang there for a moment.

Then: "But the sample looks good?"

"So far it holds up."

Logan made a little "hunh" noise. And then, sounding concerned, he said, "Looking a little disheveled there, blue boy. Fur's kinda sticking out."

"Haven't exactly had time to run a brush through it."

"Could be a sign of ill health, when an animal neglects his grooming. No offense."

"How could I possibly take offense at that?" Hank said lightly, still not looking at Logan.

"Maybe you should, y'know…take a break. Have a lie-down. Catnap. Whatever. The sample'll keep."

It was at that point that the warning bells began to sound in Hank's head. Slowly, very slowly, he looked up from the microscope at Logan, mentally noting Logan's frozen posture.

Unmoving.

Ready to pounce.

Keeping his voice carefully neutral, Hank said, "And will the sample still be here when I get back?"

Silence. Silence that spoke volumes.

Logan tossed aside any pretense of concern over Hank's health or personal grooming.

"Get rid of it. Get rid of it now, or I'll go through you to do it."

Hank stared at him, saw the way Logan was studying him. *This isn't just about the sample. I can see it in his eyes. The way he's looking at me with judgment, condemnation. As if he knew what was on my…*

…mind…

"Emma," Hank said. His eyes hardened with a sense of betrayal and violation. "She had no right to—"

"Said she couldn't help it. She said you were like a billboard. Like neon. Big neon sign flashing."

He's taking a step toward me. Trying to make it look casual. It's not casual. He's repositioning himself to allow a better angle for attack.

"And you know what she said it was flashing?" Logan continued. "Sure. Of course you know. *'I wanna get off.' 'I wanna get out.'* Is that how it goes, McCoy? You've had enough? You wanna see how the other half lives their half-lives?"

Make no sudden movements.

Hank remained in his rolling lab chair. Slowly, casually, he pivoted so as to counter Logan's stride, spoil the angle of attack. It was like a chess game. Anticipating an attack, being ready for it, was half the battle.

The other half was, of course, the battle itself.

"The truth is that I don't know what I want. And that it is none of your damn business."

Logan's brow furrowed. His eyes became slits. "Wrong answer."

He lunged. But he wasn't going for Hank. Instead his trajectory was taking him straight at the test tube with the remainder of the sample in it.

Hank had anticipated that. He whipped his chair around, brought his oversized feet into position, and thrust them upward. The move caught Logan broadside and sent him crashing up into the ceiling. The acoustical tiles crumbled from the impact, and he landed atop a counter, debris falling down around him.

"Don't push this, Logan," Hank said, working to maintain his calm even as something inside him roared to be released.

"I ain't letting you—"

"*I don't know what I am!*"

It was a painful admission, torn from the sense of shame Hank lived with constantly and could never bring himself to acknowledge. He looked down at his paws. Three clawed digits and an opposable thumb, trembling with mortification. "I used to have fingers. I used to have a mouth a woman could kiss. I would walk down the street and..." He fought to control himself and only partially succeeded, his voice growing husky. "Maybe this is the second stage of my mutation. Or maybe I'm devolving. My mind is still sharp, but my instincts, my emotions..." He forced a coarse, bitter laugh. "You, of all people, should know what it's like to be out of control."

Logan nodded ever so slightly.

The tension began to ebb out of Hank. "What am I supposed to do, Logan? Wait until I'm lying in front of the students, playing with a ball of string? *I am a human being.*"

"Wrong," was the guttural response. "You're an X-Man. We're supposed to stand for something."

He stopped as if he, too, was fighting an urge to attack. He sounded desperate to get Hank to understand. "Don't you get it? One of us caves, and it's over. You're over. Nothing good that you've ever done in your life'll matter, cause all you'll ever be is the guy who fired the starting gun for the mad dash to mutant genocide. You're one of Xavier's first students. You really wanna be on the wrong side of history? Is *that* what you want?"

"So this isn't about what *you* want," said Hank sarcastically. "You're just watching out for my best interests and my place in the mutant history books."

"You know what I want. So either flush that junk down the john right now," and Wolverine's claws snapped out, "or I'm gonna turn you into a throw rug."

Hank unleashed his own claws, protruding from the tips of his fingers, sharp, ready for blood. "Little man," he said, and the polished, calm scientific voice of Henry McCoy was gone. "*Enough!*"

They leaped toward each other, two male lions battling for the future of the pride.

They crashed into one another, each of them twisting in midair to avoid the other's claws. Hank knew the importance of keeping out of the way of

Logan's pigstickers; he was no slouch in the self-healing department, but he was hardly on Logan's level. When they hit the floor in a tangle, Logan was on the bottom. But with a twist of his hip and a fast upward thrust, Logan sent Hank tumbling backwards.

Hank allowed the momentum of the backward roll to carry him a short distance away, then sprang to his feet. But Logan was ready for him and charged. Logan was too close, the assault too quick, and there was nowhere for Hank to dodge. Logan crashed into him. The impact carried them tumbling into the hallway. Hank regained his footing first. Then, before Logan could counter the move, Hank seized the shorter man by the scruff of his neck, like an angry cat scolding a kitten, and thrust Logan's head through the opposing wall. Chunks of wood flew everywhere.

Victor Borkowski and Paras Gavaskar looked on in amazement, while the other students ran like mad.

Logan's head was momentarily stuck in the wall, but he managed to bring a foot around and kick Hank aside while he struggled to free himself.

Hank let the last vestiges of his mental control lapse. It was Hank McCoy who landed cat-like on his feet, but when Logan extricated his head and turned to face him, it was the Beast who made the charge. They went at each other again, and when they collided, the Beast's superior weight made the difference. Logan went down. The Beast's head thrust forward, roaring, saliva dripping from his bared teeth, and the only thing that stopped him from ripping out Logan's throat was the steady, determined pressure that Logan applied to push him back. As he did so, he fought to bring his Adamantium claws closer, closer to the Beast's face, hoping to inflict whatever damage he could...

Break.

The word sounded in their heads. It was not simply a message or communication. It carried with it the full weight of an irresistible order.

Instantly, unable to do anything other than obey, Logan and the Beast separated, stood up, and faced each other stiffly, their shoulders square, their hands at their sides.

And bow.

They did so, bowing deeply at the waist as if they were two martial artists who had just finished sparring. As that happened, Hank's consciousness slowly slid back to normal.

Now, continued the implacable mental commands of Emma Frost, *get into the Danger Room before I make you bloody tango.*

She allowed her mental dominance to lapse ever so slightly, just enough for them to regain control of their bodies. They glanced quickly at the students who still stood there, gaping. Then, without a word, the two men did as Emma had commanded and headed for the Danger Room.

"So…what—the teachers spend all their time here trying to kill each other?" Victor asked Paras in a low voice.

"Looks like."

Victor grinned. "This place is *so* cool."

LOGAN looked around the new environs of the Danger Room and said, "Oh, this is *really* pushing it."

Despite their recent altercation, Hank had to admit that this time he agreed with Logan.

The interior of the Danger Room had been transformed into a gigantic doll house, with Logan, Hank, Emma Frost, Scott, and Kitty the proportionate size of the dolls. The wallpaper was pink with polka dots. A tea setup on the table, with two little chairs, seemed ready for doll-sized participants. Several Brobdingnagian stuffed toys lay scattered around the room: a purple teddy bear, a blue monkey with a cheerfully stitched mouth, a cheap knock-off of Raggedy Ann, and—of all things—a Bill the Cat plush from the comic strip *Bloom County*.

"*Aack, pbthh*," muttered Hank. Logan looked at him oddly.

"I didn't program it," said Emma Frost. Hank

wasn't entirely sure he believed her, but he didn't press the matter. "But I happen to find it perfectly appropriate. I am clearly the only adult on this team."

"She's a teacher," said Kitty. "Ethics and all."

Emma didn't deign to respond. Instead she continued, "As you can see, our fearless leader has returned. Apparently he was having a nice little chat with Nick Fury."

"Cyclops to Cyclops?"

"You're a riot, Logan," said Scott. He turned his attention to Hank and Logan. "Emma's brought me up to speed on your little…"

"Teachers' conference?"

"Oh, Logan's in rare form today," said Emma. Logan tipped a little salute toward her.

Scott ignored the exchange. "Yes. On that. And on what she perceives to be your state of mind, Hank. I'm not comfortable discussing this, because I can't say I approve of the way Emma acquired this information. It shouldn't have happened."

"As I told you, Scott—" Emma began.

He didn't let her finish. "It should not. Have happened. Is that clear, Emma?"

She appeared slightly taken aback, but then reacquired her *sangfroid*. "Well, it wasn't at first, but since you broke one sentence into two and removed the contraction, that certainly clarified it, yes."

"I appreciate your understanding, Scott," said

Hank diplomatically. "Emma claims she couldn't help it. I believe her. What's done is done."

"Good. So, first things first. Hank, is your sample of the serum still viable?"

"I think so."

"When we're done here, finish your analysis. Let's not be tearing each other apart over a fake."

"And if it works?" Logan looked at him sidelong, his gaze filled with suspicion.

Hank wasn't inclined to answer.

"If it does," Scott said, "then I'm trusting you not to do anything till you've spoken to me. I have to say I'm with Logan on this. But I'm just asking that we talk. Is that fair?"

Hank didn't reply, but he couldn't keep the feeling of betrayal out of his eyes. Scott Summers was one of his oldest, closest friends. They'd been together since the beginning. Back in the days when Hank had been so insecure that he felt compelled to show off his intellect at every occasion, always using polysyllabic phrases instead of simple words. Back when they were young, and Professor X was running the show, and Jean was alive, and everything seemed possible. Back when he wasn't a furred...

...freak...

"What did Fury say?" asked Hank.

Scott's fleeting expression showed that he was

perfectly aware Hank had sidestepped his question. Choosing not to pursue it, he outlined in broad strokes the specifics of his conversation with the head of S.H.I.E.L.D. "Long story short," he concluded, "we're on our own. Either Nick Fury has joined the ranks of the mutant-hating masses...or he's hiding an agenda. Either way, we shouldn't expect any help from the government."

"*There's* a surprise," said Logan. He was slumped against the purple teddy bear, the oversized heart on its chest serving as a whimsical contrast.

"What about the Professor?" said Kitty. "Do you think he knows what's happening? Why isn't he here weighing in? Giving us some direction?"

Emma sat demurely in one of the chairs at the table, eyeing the plastic tea service thoughtfully. "Because he's half a world away in Genosha, working with other mutants. And I would hope, since he's trusting us to run this team, that he assumes we're not about to go whimpering to him for help at the first sign of a crisis." Almost as an afterthought, she looked to Scott to back her up. "Scott?" she prompted when he failed to respond immediately.

"Uh...yes, I agree," said Scott, looking like he'd just been roused from a stupor. "Um...Kitty, you're our computer whiz. Start running down Benetech. I want to know exactly who's funding this research.

Hank, you'll be in your lab. Emma, check the students. See whether any have come wandering back, and if any others are thinking of bolting. If nothing else, we have a duty to their parents to keep track of them. I'll contact some of the other teams, some of the more far-flung mutants, see how far this is reaching."

"And me?" said Logan.

"Have a beer. And stay away from Hank."

Logan nodded approvingly. "It's a plan."

Hank, Logan, and Kitty headed for the door, Hank and Logan keeping a wary distance from each other. Kitty asked Logan cautiously, "Are you gonna fight everyone, Logan? I just wanna know if I'm next."

"Nah," he said. "You'd go ninja on me. I can't take that kind of hurt."

As they walked out, Scott allowed his frustration to show a bit. "We're getting nowhere, Emma."

"Patience, darling," she said soothingly. "You're doing fine. Of course, Kitty thinks I'm mentally controlling everything you say."

Scott smiled at the notion. Then he frowned, turned to her and said, "But you're *not*, right?"

Making no effort to hide her annoyance, Emma said, "You will never see me naked again."

* * * *

SCOTT and Emma lay in bed that night. Emma was making good on her threat, but Scott thought he might be able to dissuade her from holding firm to it. Then there came a banging on the door. Scott answered only to see, to his surprise, a quietly furious Hank McCoy.

Scott's first thought was a natural one: *Oh God, what did Logan do now?* So he was somewhat surprised when Hank said brusquely, "We have to go to Benetech. Now, tonight."

It took Scott a moment to reorient himself. "The cure...it's real? It's...what? Dangerous?"

"It's not about that. It's about the body they're running their tests on."

"I don't understand...body...?"

"Their cure, they..." He gestured helplessly. "They made it sound like they developed it in a lab, tested it on Tildie Soames, and lo and behold, they were good to go. I should have known better. My own desire to see this as some sort of miracle, handed down by the same gods who made us what we are... who made me what I am..."

"Hank, you're not making a tremendous amount of sense."

"It was tested on, and developed with, the DNA of other mutants. It's the only explanation."

Scott and Emma exchanged appalled looks. "Other mutants? Being held against their will?"

"Dead mutants, Scott. Dead, and their corpses are being utilized to further the research that would bring an end to their own kind. Mutants who…" He hesitated, clearly horrified at the very concept. "Why does nothing ever stay buried?"

Scott couldn't even ask the next question.

Emma did it for him. "Any dead mutants we know?"

She didn't have to speak the name. It was there, right in front of them, the ever-present ghost that haunted all their lives.

"Jean," said Scott.

FOURTEEN

—————— ✦ ——————

"JET'S prepped," Cyclops said briskly as he walked across the hangar bay.

Beast was already in his uniform, and Emma was pulling on her long white gloves. "The others are coming," said Beast.

"You didn't say anything to...?" Cyclops' voice trailed off.

"Of course not. I told them Benetech *might* be using *a* mutant for tissue samples. That's all. I didn't specify."

"Because we probably won't find anything conclusive," said Cyclops.

Emma lanced him with a look. "Like a warm body?"

Before Scott could answer, Wolverine and Kitty entered. Lockheed sat perched on Kitty's shoulder, looking a bit annoyed at being roused in the middle of the night.

"Good to go," said Wolverine. He looked pleased at the opportunity to create some mayhem for the very individuals who had turned his world upside down. He cast a quick look toward Beast that seemed to say: *Told you so. I knew these Benetech goons weren't right guys.* Then he walked straight past the others and toward the Blackbird. "Let's bring on some hurt."

"This is recon, Logan," Cyclops advised him. "Until we know what we're dealing with, we're just looking."

"We know what we're dealing with, Summers." He cast one final glance over his shoulder before he boarded the plane. "Animals."

Minutes later the Blackbird was soaring through the sky. The moon was full, so an ordinary plane would have had very little chance of masking its presence. But the Blackbird was outfitted with holographic camouflage technology. When the plane approached Benetech, it was not only as black as the night sky, but there were small twinkling effects along its hull, mimicking the stars above it. The only time it was visible was when it briefly flew past the moon, and then only for a second or two.

"Scott. Look," said the Beast, gesturing toward the ground.

Cyclops had to squint to see what came so easily to Beast's eyesight. A mass of people were gathered outside, many of them lying on blankets spread on solid sidewalks. Some had pitched tents. Most were asleep, but some were still moving around, apparently engaged in animated discussions.

"What do you think they're talking about?" the Beast wondered aloud. "Purity of vision? The destiny of the mutant race? How exciting it will be to walk down the street without attracting stares? How eager they are to live a normal life?"

"So now you're deciding what's normal?" said Wolverine from nearby. "Who are you to do that?"

"Who are we to decide on their behalf?" said Beast.

"We're the guys who are raiding Benetech to find out how much blood is on the hands of—"

"The Knicks," said Emma.

They all looked at her. "What?" said a bewildered Cyclops.

"The people down there. They're having an endlessly juvenile discussion about the Knicks game tonight. I listened only briefly because I could feel myself hemorrhaging IQ points."

There was dead silence.

"Knicks *were* on fire tonight," Wolverine finally said.

"Hell yes," Kitty agreed. "Did you believe that half-court shot in the third quarter—?"

Emma stared at her, appalled.

"What?" said Kitty defensively. "I can't have layers?"

Cyclops decided to ignore the entire exchange. He focused on looking for a safe landing area, sufficiently far away from Benetech to avoid detection. There was no way they were going to be able to set down on the grounds themselves, but Benetech's blossoming success in recent years meant that a section of forest nearby was being cleared to expand the facility. At the moment the construction area consisted of a large, flat expanse that would serve perfectly. The Blackbird reached its landing point, hovered, and then descended straight down.

Once they had settled, Cyclops powered down the plane and said, "Kitty's on point."

"The canary in the coal mine. I'm game. What do I do?"

"They've got the deluxe detection package in there, so you'll want to start from below."

"We can't just go in the way Hank did when he went to talk to Doctor Rao?"

Beast shook his head. "That path was more or less unique to my particular skill set. Plus we have to assume they've ramped things up security-wise since my visit, so we couldn't retrace that way even if we wanted to. Security mainframe should be housed in the basement, according to the computer files you were gracious enough to hack into for me."

"Glad I could help the team."

"Think you can disable it without tripping anything?" said Beast.

She nodded. "It's done."

"When do *I* get to disable something?" Logan asked.

Emma rolled her eyes. "Oh, sheathe it, will you? Inspiring costumes notwithstanding, we're not heroes tonight. Let's try to be subtle for once."

"Actually," said Kitty, "I could use him as backup."

"Fine. But keep him on a leash."

LEONARD Tucker was still called "Sarge" even though his police days were long past him. A bullet in the leg had rendered him unfit for duty, so he'd been forced to take a job as a security guard. But he'd quickly risen to the top of the pecking order with his cool confidence and ability to adapt to any situation quickly and efficiently. A natural leader of men, he'd been placed in charge of a three-person team assigned to guard the heart of the company's entire security system, the mainframe down in what was referred to as the dungeon.

The facility was on high alert already because of all the damned mutants outside. Tucker had begged corporate for the opportunity to take a squad out and rid the place of them. They had no business being

there. Sure, they were looking for a cure to their condition, but so what? Life was tough all over. It didn't
excuse trespassing or loitering. Corporate, unfortunately, had put the kibosh on that idea. They were
concerned over the way it would play on national television, desperate people being dragged away against
their will, treated violently simply because they
wanted to be normal.

It annoyed the crap out of him. Tucker was, by
nature, territorial, and he didn't want these mutants
around. Especially when, for all he knew, they might
at any point become sick of simply waiting and make
a full-blown charge on the gate. Considering the
power they were packing, there was little doubt in
Tucker's mind that they'd be able to break through,
and then the guards would have a real fight on their
hands. Better to clear the mutants out now while they
were still peaceful, still hopeful, still vulnerable.

He was telling all this to Jenkins, his second in
command, as they stood near the monitor system,
keeping a wary eye on the screens. The mutants stood
outside, not budging, not causing any problems.

"Expecting trouble, Sarge?" said Jenkins, nodding toward the rifle Tucker had tucked leisurely under his arm.

"Always," said Tucker. "Especially now. We have
to keep our weapons at hand, because these mutants...they *are* their weapons. They don't have to go

for it; it's right there in their eyes or mouths or arms or whatever, ready to be—"

All the screens flickered at the exact same moment. It was so subtle that anyone else might not have noticed it at all. But the movement instantly caught Tucker's eye. He stared at the monitors, studying them.

"Sarge?"

Tucker didn't reply. Something was wrong. Something was strange. Something was—

"There. That mutant right there." He pointed to one of the monitors, which showed a mutant with scales like a fish. "The one who's walking from the left side of the screen to the right, and then sitting down?"

"Yeah. What about him?" said Jenkins.

"He was already sitting on the right. Just a minute ago."

"Are you sure? I don't think he—"

Tucker wasn't listening. He moved past the bank of screens to the guts of the system. Jenkins followed him.

They rounded the corner and stopped dead.

A young woman wearing a blue-and-gold uniform, her hair back in a ponytail, was standing *inside* the computer banks. Her upper body emerged ghost-like from a console. Her fingers darted across a keyboard. She froze in position when she saw the two guards crouched, their weapons leveled at her.

"Oh. Hi," she said pleasantly. "Saw me implementing the loop, huh? I knew there was a chance of that."

"Jenkins, sound a full security alert!" shouted Tucker.

"Good luck with that," she said.

Something struck Jenkins from behind. He went down without a word, sprawling on his face. A low moan indicated he was still conscious.

Tucker whirled and saw some manner of creature in the shadows. It seemed to be holding knives in either hand, and a feral joy showed on its face.

"Say hello to my little friend," said the girl cheerily.

Tucker swung his rifle up. The knives sliced through the air and through the weapon, sending the entire front section clattering to the floor. Tucker stared down in shock at the destroyed rifle, and then a fist hit him in the face. It was like being struck by a mallet. His legs went out from under him and he collapsed. As the world turned black around him, he heard Jenkins shout a warning, followed by the sounds of metal striking metal and a bone-crunching blow. A body hit the floor...Jenkins, he suspected. Then Tucker was unconscious.

When he came to, hours later, everything was long over.

* * * *

CYCLOPS, Beast, and Emma stood at the rendez-vous point outside the back of the vast Benetech complex. Situated near the edge of what had once been a copious forest, it was relatively secluded, the building itself providing cover courtesy of lengthy shadows. This side of the fifteen-story building was devoid of windows: nothing but solid wall from top to bottom, giving it almost the appearance of a warehouse.

"Not much for décor, are they?" said Emma.

"Typical for a facility like this," the Beast said. "This section is likely where they do their serious R&D work. Windows provide vulnerability for spying. Of course, limited sighting means that miscreants like us sneak up unseen, which is why they have those." He pointed at a camera mounted on a pole directly overhead. "With any luck, however, Kitty has managed to attend to that."

"No alarms have been triggered," said Cyclops, "so that's a good sign."

Then Kitty emerged, passing through the outer wall. "Okay. Who's first?"

"Let's do it," said Beast. He held out his hand.

Lockheed fluttered through the air and landed on Kitty's shoulder. She smiled when she saw him and said, "Sure, buddy, I can take you, too. Let's go." Kitty, Beast, and Lockheed then melted into the wall, leaving no trace behind.

"Wait...*that's* the plan?" said Emma. "Nobody told

me that was the plan, having her phase through the wall with us like spectral hitchhikers."

"How did you *think* we were going to get in?" said Cyclops.

"Through a door, like normal people."

"Doors are two-way. Someone might be coming out as we're going in, and they could sound an alarm."

"We could have Henry eat them."

"See, Emma, it's suggestions like that that make me reluctant to take you nice places."

Kitty reemerged from the wall and said, "Okay... who's next?"

Emma stood there, unmoving. Cyclops shrugged and walked toward Kitty. She took him by the elbow and they vanished into the wall. Emma watched them go, contemplated her situation for a bit, and then said quietly, "To hell with this." She turned to head back away from the building.

"Going somewhere, Miss Frost? Certainly you're not scared of trusting a naïve little half-wit like me?" Emma turned to see Kitty, extending her hand in a sweet, mock-innocent manner.

"How do I know I can trust you?" said Emma.

"Because I *know* I can't trust you, and you're aware it's my goal in life to be, in every way, the complete opposite of you."

Emma considered for a moment, then nodded. "Actually, that makes sense."

She took Kitty's hand. Seconds later, they were gliding through darkness and substance.

Emma felt completely disoriented. She had no idea where she was, or in what direction she was going. Her survival instincts kicked in, and instinctively she tried to pull away from Kitty. Kitty reached over with her free hand and firmly gripped Emma's forearm, thwarting her attempt to get away. To Emma, it seemed as if Kitty were pulling her down, down into a bottomless pit, where Kitty could just let go and be rid of the dreaded and hated Emma Frost once and for all...

And suddenly they emerged into a basement, wall-to-wall metal, with console arrays and screens lined up along the walls, displaying security readouts. Conical overhead lamps provided illumination, casting a haze of green over the entire area where Cyclops, Beast, and Lockheed were waiting for them. Beast was saying, "Place is a bit of a maze, but the main research center is definitely up top."

The moment they fully emerged into the room, Emma pulled away from Kitty. "God, but that is unnerving," said Emma.

"Wriggle like that next time," Kitty warned her, "and I'll lose my grip in the middle of a wall. You'll fuse molecules. As deaths go, it's not the funnest."

"Thanks for the safety tip."

Wolverine emerged from the back. "Found two

more guards besides the ones we already ran into. They came over all sleepy just now."

"Will they ever wake up?" Kitty said cautiously.

"Probably," said Wolverine. "No promises, though."

"Teams," Cyclops said briskly. "We work every floor. Emma with me. Kitty with Lockheed. Which leaves the Hardy Boys: Beast, Wolverine, think you can avoid killing each other long enough for us to help other people?"

They looked at each other briefly, then nodded.

"Let's do it," said Cyclops. "Emma will be monitoring everyone. If you have anything to report…"

"Think happy thoughts?" said Kitty brightly.

"Something like that."

CYCLOPS was going through the files in one room, trying to find some sort of specific reference to the project they were searching for, when he slowly became aware that Emma wasn't helping. He turned and, sure enough, she was simply standing there, leaning against a file cabinet, her right foot propped against a drawer. Had this been a scene out of *film noir*, she'd have been taking a slow drag on a cigarette.

"You know, this would take half as long if we were both doing it," he said.

Emma did nothing. Mentally shrugging, Cyclops went back to work. After a time, she finally spoke: "What happens if she's alive?"

"What?" He looked at Emma in confusion. "She's not. She's dead. I was there when she died."

"And her coming back from the dead is *utterly* without precedent. I say again: What happens?"

"I don't understand what you—"

Her eyes glittered, hard like the diamond she was capable of transforming into. "What happens to us? Are we done? Do you expect me to just step aside?"

He was silent.

She pressed the question. "Do you want me to pretend your heart doesn't race when you think of her?"

"She's a part of me, Emma. Comes with the package, as you know."

"And that brings us back to the question of what happens to us." Before he could reply, she continued, "Just so we're clear: The A answer is, 'I love you, Emma, and nothing will change that.' The B answer is, 'We'll cross that bridge when we come to it.' The C answer of a threesome is, frankly, a non-starter."

Leaving open a file drawer, he walked over to her and stared at her with his usual stoic expression. "You're Emma Frost. Since when do you wait for others to tell you how things are going to be?"

Her chin trembled ever so slightly, and then she quickly got it under control. "Apparently since now."

He put his hand on the back of her head, drew her mouth to his and kissed her with a ferocity that belied his usual detached manner. It went on for long moments and when their lips finally parted, he said softly, "Where does that answer rate?"

"Jury's still out," she said.

He actually chuckled as he turned away from her, returning to the task at hand. "You're a piece of work, Emma."

She pulled open a drawer to start aiding in the search. "You have *no* idea," she said softly.

WOLVERINE and Beast made their way stealthily through the cross corridors. Using their combined hyper-senses, agility, and tendency to blend well with shadows, they'd made it up to the tenth floor without being detected.

Standing at the end of a long corridor, Wolverine said abruptly, "I'm not lovin' this. It's too easy. There's hardly anyone around."

"It's after hours."

"Yeah, and they're working hellbent for leather on Miracle, *and* they got a bunch of mutants at the gates. You'd think the whole place would be humming."

"You're implying that this might be—?"

"A setup? That since you came in here solo, they

figured we might bring a whole raiding party, and prepped for it? Yeah, it occurred to me."

"So you're saying we should get out?"

"Hell no. I'm sayin' bring 'em on."

"Fantastic. By the way, I missed something. You mentioned 'Miracle.' Who's that? Sounds like a race horse."

"That's what they're calling the cure now. 'Miracle.' It was on the news. Catchy, eh?"

Beast did not reply.

Wolverine paused at an intersection, sniffed the air to make certain they were alone, and then headed to the right. Beast followed him.

"So what's your personal miracle?" Wolverine continued. "Lose the fur…nice girl, couple of kids and a teaching job somewhere that doesn't get blown up too often?"

"You're not exactly talking me out of it there, Logan."

"You think I don't get it?"

"That's exactly what I think, yes."

"Yeah, well, you're wrong." He stopped for a moment, but didn't turn to face the Beast. "Nothing wrong with wanting the whole wife-and-kids package. It's the part where you sit on the couch with the family and watch on TV while every mutant on the face of the Earth gets lined up. Get a little Miracle or get a lot dead."

"Right, right, and then I get to boast to the kids how I helped kick off the beginnings of our own private holocaust. Just how much guilt do you really need to heap on—"

"Quiet."

"Not to sound juvenile, but you started it…"

"No, I mean it: Hold it. You catch that scent?"

The Beast's nostrils flared. "Female."

"Dead," Wolverine added.

"Emma?" Beast said. He could have just thought at her, but he found it focused him to speak aloud.

I have you, Emma thought back at him. *You're on the tenth floor, Section 1138. On our way.*

CYCLOPS and Emma were one floor down and on the opposite side of the building when they received Beast's call. In their haste to reach Wolverine and Beast, they ran up against several Benetech employees. Emma was brisk and ruthless in her handling of them. Two research scientists became obsessed with a book of Sudoku. A guard grabbed the nearest computer station and started surfing the web for porn.

"That one was too easy," Emma told Scott.

They reached a room from within which a pale green light was shining. "I'm having trouble locking on to Kitty," said Emma. "You go on in; I'll stay out here where it's quieter so I can better focus."

Cyclops nodded. Then he braced himself and pushed open the door.

Wolverine stood on the far side of a table in the middle of the room, an array of fluorescent lights shining down. Beast was at the end of the table.

A female body was laid out, draped in a blanket. On either side of her, luminescent wings spilled over the edges of the table. In life they had doubtless been lovely, shimmering—living incarnations of pure beauty. Now they just hung loosely, useless and faded shadows of themselves.

The girl herself had pale, orange skin, festooned with blue markings that appeared to be an elaborate set of tattoos. That, or she had developed them naturally as part of a secondary mutation. Not that it mattered anymore. She was long gone.

"We don't know her," Wolverine said.

Beast pointed to red markings just above her hands. "Striations on her wrists would indicate she took her own life."

Wolverine adjusted the blanket, making sure to fully cover the naked girl. "Or someone made it look like she did…"

"Frankly, I don't care whether or not they had anything to do with her death. This is sickening," said Beast.

Wolverine nodded, pleased that he and Beast seemed to be on the same page at last. Who, after all, would be willing to trust their fate to the cure—even benefit from it—if the cost of that benefit was the lives of innocent people such as this poor, unnamed girl? "It's all here, people," Wolverine said. "The cure. These little experiments. One well-aimed missile from the jet and we all sleep easy."

"We can't torch Benetech, Logan," said Cyclops. "We still don't know everything. This can't be the only body."

"So you're saying that after we do know every-thing we *can* torch…" Then Wolverine's voice trailed off as something in Cyclops' tone caught his notice. "Wait. Why can't this be the only body? What are we after here?" When they didn't respond, his jaw visibly tightened. "You two better tell me what's going on. As in now."

Before either Cyclops or Beast could reply, Emma pushed the door open. "I still can't reach Kitty. I don't think she's in the building."

"Where would she go?" asked Cyclops.

Suddenly, Emma doubled over in pain. A stran-gled *gnaaaah* issued from her throat. Cyclops barely got to her in time before she collapsed completely. "Emma—?"

"It's my girls…the Stepford Cuckoos…" she man-aged to whisper. "They're calling me. It's so loud. I can't make it out…Scott," and she looked up at him with rare fear and desperation in her eyes. "We have to get back."

Then bullets began exploding all around them.

Cyclops was closest to the door. He couldn't see the attackers clearly, but the effectiveness of their weaponry couldn't be denied. He would have been killed instantly, even with the reinforced mesh of his costume, but Wolverine saved him, leaping in and knocking both Cyclops and Emma out of the way.

A barrage of bullets struck Wolverine in midair. It wasn't enough to kill him. Oftentimes, it seemed nothing was. It did, however, cause him to cry out in agony as he writhed, but did not fall, under the assult.

The Beast was too far away to help and too close to withstand a direct hit. He leaped aside, seeking shelter, as bullets winged past him.

One of the bullets ricocheted off Wolverine and struck Cyclops across the back, just above the shoulder blades. He went down. Emma cried out his name.

"I'm just tagged," he managed to get out. Struggling to raise his voice above the chatter of bullets, he said, "X-Men…sound…sound off…"

Instantly, Emma transformed into her diamond form and turned to face her opponents, her face twisted in pure fury.

The men who had now entered the room were not the least bit intimidated. Emma could see now that there were three of them, the upper parts of their bodies covered in plated armor, and they were wearing helmets with high-tech earpieces covering either side of their heads. The arm pieces that extended from their reinforced shoulders were very large, because of what was mounted over their forearms: massive, high-powered multi-barreled guns, cyclical in design. The high-speed rotary weapons were clearly capable of spitting out hundreds of rounds per minute. Emma made no move.

Her attention was entirely on Cyclops.

"Sound off," he whispered again as the floor beneath him began to pool with blood.

Emma eased into his mind.

He is surrounded by a delirious assortment of figures. It is impossible for Emma to see clearly what any of them look like; they are little more than shades, vague forms given substance. They are nothing more than half-finished thoughts, dream re-creations of people he had once encountered who had no meaning to him at the time, but assumed new and unwarranted importance now.

They say nonsensical things.

"Iceman, sounding off."

"Fireman, sounding off."

"Clothing-Man, sounding off."

"Ability-to-Hop-Man, here."

"Wait a minute," Scott says, "Aren't you all the same person?"

"Oh Scott. Oh darling," and sure enough, there she is, the energy-wielding destroyer of Emma's happiness, Jean-freaking-Grey. Never far from his thoughts, even possibly his dying ones. She hovers over him, her arms

spread to either side, her legs straight, as if she has just been crucified. She is fearsome in her beauty, surrounded by a corona of flame, a living sun descending to incinerate her worshipper. Her red hair is spread in all directions, crackling like a burning crown. Her eyes are empty yellow and her beauty is terrible to see. Likewise terrible are her words: "What a failure you are."

"No...no, I got this wired," Scott protests. "I'm putting in storm windows."

"Oh, seriously..."

"Do we have to do this in front of everybody?"

Jean leans in, floating over him. "Stop faking it, Scott. I did."

"Jean, please...just tell me...do you at least like the costumes?"

All of this passes through Scott's head with literally the speed of thought. The figures register as little more than vague impressions in the back of Emma's psychic eye, and only her mental acuity allows her to discern them individually for what they are. Less than one second of real time has passed, yet Emma has already seen more than enough.

Then Emma slapped him across the face. "Stay awake, Scott!"

She turned to face the men, the ones with guns for hands. "He's bleeding out. He needs medical attention. *Now.*"

It was a command, sent straight into their heads.

They smiled and did nothing to obey. Emma realized: They must have the same sort of scramblers in their heads as the mercs did, the ones she'd fought back in the penthouse. The fact that they had access to the same technology was of interest to Emma. But at the moment, all that really mattered was saving the life of Scott Summers.

"Bleeding out," the leader of the squad said indifferently. "Really. Glad I'm not him, then."

FIFTEEN

———————— 🜨 ————————

TWENTY *minutes earlier…*

"Man, I'm glad I'm not you."

Hisako had pulled an all-nighter studying, and was finally ready to go to bed. Emerging from the girls' locker room, freshly showered and wearing pink pajamas, she was surprised to find Edward literally just floating aimlessly around the place. Everyone knew about his fight with Jay. The students' opinions, whose side they were on, pretty much fell along the lines of how they felt about the mutant cure itself.

But Edward had also been hit with major-league detention and sanctions having nothing to do with the actual fight. No one had known exactly why, until Edward now confessed the truth of it to Hisako.

"No wonder you got detention, you loser," she continued as she walked down the hall, Edward drifting along above her. "Miss Pryde's a teacher! Just 'cause you've got the hots for her doesn't make you equals. You can't call her an idiot!"

"She just got me so mad! That patronizing line that mutants are all gonna stick together. I mean, she's fought some of the what do you mean 'hots'?"

"Oh, please. Like there's five guys on campus who aren't crushing on her. '*Ooh,*'" and she pitched her voice into a fair approximation of Kitty's. "'*I'm a real X-Man only I'm young and cool and I know all about computers and maybe a cute senior would have a shot with me if he seemed really sensitive and super-powered...*' That, and variations on that, are what every stupid boy in this place is hoping that Miss Pryde's thinking."

"You're a mind reader, Hisako," he said sarcastically.

"No, but Blindfold is."

Edward was taken aback. He hadn't been wild about Blindfold since he'd first encountered her. Her real name was Ruth Aldine, but the code name "Blindfold" had been a natural one since the raven-haired young woman always wore an actual blindfold tied across her face. Between that and her tendency to wear fringed shawls and stand around looking omniscient (which, considering her proclivity for telepathy, clairvoyance, and precognition, she more or less was), Edward felt she was working too hard to make an impression. So she was blind: Let her get a cane and sunglasses and get over herself.

Now, though, he was being given firsthand evidence that his automatic dislike for her wasn't entirely personal. This was clearly someone who couldn't be trusted.

"She's *reading* the guys' *minds*?" he asked, appalled. "That's so against the bylaws."

"She also said the only reason you came here was you wanna make X-Man."

"What? That...that is so—"

"You don't have to get all defensive, Edward. Not with me. You wanna be an X-Man? Join the club. Apart from the losers lining up for that bogus cure, who doesn't wanna make the A-list?"

Edward drifted to the ground and touched down lightly. "Blindfold. Sheesh. No eyes, big mouth."

"She's a blabber, yeah," admitted Hisako. "But she's okay. I just think she's really lonely. I mean, think about it for a minute..."

And then they stopped dead.

A massive armored figure stood directly in front of them, blocking their path.

"Minute's up," he rumbled.

The two of them stared at him, confused. "Uh... who are you?" said Edward.

"I? I am Ord of the Breakworld." He paused. "And you are—?"

Edward and Hisako exchanged looks. "I'm...
Wing." It seemed right that when some big armored
guy was in front of him, he should give his code name.
"And this is..." He hesitated. "Do you have a code
name yet?"

"Armor." It was all Hisako said, and she did so
flatly and without emotion. Her arms hung loosely,
ready to move, and she was balanced lightly on the
balls of her feet. In short, she had subtly assumed a
defensive posture, ready to react to an assault.

Edward didn't notice. He was trying to determine
what this new guy's deal was. "Uhm...are you a friend
of the X-Men?"

"More an acquaintance. Bring them to me." It was
not a request.

"They're not here."

"Not here." He sounded vaguely put out. "Are you
quite sure?"

"Positive. I saw the X-plane take off like two
hours ago."

"And you don't know where they went?"

Edward shook his head. "A mission or something.
I mean, they don't tell us stuff like that."

"This is very frustrating."

"Did you wanna leave them a message?" Edward
said helpfully.Something in the phrasing seemed to
catch Ord's attention. He stared at them as if truly
seeing them for the first time. "You two are mutants."

"But we're not, like, cool ones or anything," said Edward.

"Wing…" Hisako said warningly.

"Wing, you have given me an excellent idea," said Ord. "And you have my thanks for that. I believe I will leave the X-Men a message."

He brought up his right fist. Three hypodermic needles snapped out from a holster on the glove.

HISAKO had picked up on their danger before Edward had. *He's so trusting. I really liked that about him. Now I hate him for it.*

When Edward had suggested leaving a message, she saw the way that this "Ord" had looked at him. She didn't have to be a telepath to know what was suddenly going through his mind. The naïve Wing still wasn't seeing it, didn't realize what was about to happen. Hisako closed her eyes tightly in concentration, slowed down her breathing, and tried to stop her heart from racing. The fight-or-flight impulse surged in her, and she used the few seconds she had between threat and attack to get the "flight" part under control. The microsecond that the threat became explicit, when those terrifying hypos snapped out of Ord's fingertips, Wing was flatfooted with shock, but Hisako was ready. "Wing…*get out!*"

With those last two words, as she screamed at the top of her lungs, Hisako's energy field flashed into existence around her. She put all her resolve, all her focus, into her head and arms, strengthening the field around those parts of her. Her armored right fist whipped around, and she caught Ord in the stomach. It was a sloppy punch, unfocused, desperate, thrown by a young girl not yet fully trained in her abilities. It was, however, sufficient to send Ord flying backwards onto the floor.

Wing stood frozen, despite Hisako's urging that he get out of there as quickly as possible.

She was completely enveloped in her psionic armor now, and she lunged toward Ord. "Congratulations," he said, lashing out with his feet. His kick sent her crashing back into the wall, which shattered from the impact. "You startled me."

Then Ord rose, not so much standing up as uncoiling. "Now...boy," he said, moving forward toward Wing.

WING snapped out of his paralysis. A window hung open behind him. He threw himself backwards and out, and seconds later he was hurtling straight up into the night sky.

His mind was racing, filled with confusion and humiliation. His first real call to battle, and in the face of a genuine opponent, Hisako had stepped up, while all he could manage to do was fly the coop.

High in the air, he floated. "Hisako," he said mournfully to himself. "What am I doing? I can't just leave her there." He couldn't abandon her, he realized. He had to go back to face—

And suddenly there was a rushing of air and a massive weight landed on his back. "I was talking to you, boy," came the snarling voice of Ord.

Wing desperately tried to pull away, but he had no chance. Ord effortlessly kept him right where he was, and Wing felt a stabbing pain in his back. A pain that he would remember for the rest of his life, however long or short that might be. A pain that spelled the beginning of the end.

He shrieked in high-pitched agony, and then Ord whipped him around and stared into his face. "Now you will give them my message. That the mutant abomination will never be a threat to the Breakworld. That man was not meant to fly."

And with that pronouncement, he hurled Wing toward the ground.

HISAKO hadn't been knocked out, just stunned. Her psionic armor remained in place. Sitting up, she looked around frantically but saw no sign of Ord. *He had me on the ropes; why didn't he finish—?*

Then she heard a scream from outside and above.

Seeing the window hanging open, she instantly put two and two together. She clambered through it, searching the skies desperately, and then she spotted him.

Wing was plummeting like a fallen angel. He tumbled over and over, waving his arms frantically as if he could actually flap them. There was no sign of Ord anywhere; apparently he'd taken off.

At that moment, Ord's presence was the least of Hisako's worries. She ran as fast as she could, the extra-long legs of her armor providing her with greater speed. But Wing was falling horribly fast, and she was terrified she wasn't going to get to him.

He screamed all the way down, the most horrible, soul-wrenching sound Hisako had ever heard. She tried to stretch her armor, make it even bigger, and then she was out of time and she leaped as far as she could. Twisting in midair, she landed flat on her back, praying she could cushion the fall.

Wing crash-landed into her. Had she not been armored up, the impact would have crushed both of them. As it was, she felt nothing, but she heard a sickening crunch. Wing rebounded off her and would have struck the ground, but she managed to reach out with her huge armored arms and catch him.

Then she was on her feet and running toward the school. She knew she shouldn't move an accident victim, but she had no choice. The priority was getting him to the one person who could help him while he was still alive.

She ran in through the side door, shouting, "*Elixir! Elixir!*" at the top of her lungs.

He wasn't around. The Stepford Cuckoos, however, were. The three slender blonde teens, clad in identical red bathrobes, all shared the same pale complexion of Emma Frost, but the cold cynicism that often seemed present in Emma's eyes was absent from theirs. They tended to lean toward one another when they were seen together, which was most of the time. They really were indistinguishable; even their shoulder-length blonde hair was mussed in exactly the same manner. They gazed at Hisako with their usual detached curiosity.

"Get Elixir down here," Hisako ordered them.

The Cuckoos nodded slightly in unison and closed their eyes. Seconds later there was a yelp from an upstairs bedroom, followed by a hurried thudding of feet. Elixir sprinted down the front stairs, bellowing, "Where do you three get off showing up in my dream—?"

Then he stopped, his eyes widening as he saw Wing's battered and broken body.

Instantly Elixir was all business. "Lie him down on the couch," he said, pointing to the den. "How the hell did this happen?"

Hisako told him as quickly as she could. Elixir laid his hands on Wing, who was barely breathing.

"Celeste, Mindee, Phoebe…get in touch with Miss Frost. Tell her to get back here; we're under attack."

"He called himself Ord," said Hisako. "At the moment, he's gone."

Elixir nodded but added grimly, "And he could return any time, I take it?"

"God, I hope not."

The three blonde girls—or the three-in-one, as they were often referred to—tilted their heads toward each other, communing together to focus their abilities. They spoke in such closely overlapping sentences that it was impossible to tell where one of their minds ended and the next one began. "*She is far away, but we will do our best.*"

"Is…" Hisako was almost afraid to ask. "Is he going to be okay?"

Elixir continued to pour his healing energy into Wing. "I want to get him stabilized enough so we can move him over to the infirmary. These are bad breaks, but I'm working on it. Your armor's not exactly fluffy, Hisako."

"It was all so…so fast…if only I could have softened the armor to cushion his fall more."

"Don't blame yourself. If you hadn't caught him at all, he'd have been a fruit smoothie. You did great."

"I don't feel great."

The Cuckoos suddenly spoke up, one to the next to the next continuously, together but separate. "*We reached Miss Frost, but she has broken contact. Something is happening where she is./Something about Mister Summers./She's horribly in love with him./Love is the stupidest thing I ever heard of./Her thoughts about him during class are often sweaty and inappropriate."*

This was not what Hisako wanted or needed to hear. "Okay, you guys wanna stay with us here? Can you reach anyone else?"

"Not at this distance. We have a special bond with—/What about Blindfold? Doesn't she read—?"

At that moment there was a low moan behind Hisako. She spun and saw, to her joy, that Edward was sitting up. He was bruised, but his limbs weren't pointing in any unnatural directions and he didn't appear to be bleeding, at least not externally.

Elixir had removed his hands from Edward and was nodding in satisfaction. "He should be cool," he said.

"Wing! Are you hurt?"

"Hisako?" He was clearly disoriented. "What did I—?"

"That Ord guy knocked you out."

Edward frowned, apparently putting back together the pieces of what he'd experienced. And then slow, dawning terror began to appear in his face. "Oh God. Oh no. My powers...oh God..."

Hisako knew. Deep down she knew, but was too appalled to say it out loud. Instead she said, "Wing? What's wrong?" She prayed desperately that she was wrong, that it was something else entirely.

But she was right.

Looking up at her like a crippled sparrow, Wing whispered, "I'm cured."

———————— 🗲 ————————

You know how they say, "Trust your instincts"? I'm pretty much the poster girl for that.

I can sense the density of the world around me, but damned if I know how I do it. Hank would probably call it a "secondary mutation." A side effect of my ability to pass through solid objects. A subliminal way of knowing what I'm getting myself into.

So while the others are heading off in different directions, to search Benetech from top to bottom, I suddenly realize that the "bottom" of this place might not be what we think it is at all.

We're in the subbasement. Below me should be nothing but foundation or earth. Yet I can sense more construction beneath my feet. Storage? Secret lab? Something else entirely? What is it and how can I get to it?

I could spend long minutes running around, trying to find an elevator. But I might wind up just wasting time, which I can't afford to do since I don't know how much time we have left. And besides—and I'm not proud of myself, but

I smirk when I think this—that's what Emma would have to do. I have a simpler way, and not only is it something she couldn't do, but she wouldn't have the nerve to try it along with me.

It's a cheap and petty triumph, not to mention mostly in my own head. But I'll take my wins where I can get them.

I sink up to my waist experimentally. There's nothing beneath my feet except metal. It just keeps going down. Weird. I point commandingly at Lockheed. "You stay here and don't eat anyone. I'm gonna check it out."

Then I vanish into the floor and begin my descent.

Nothing but blackness all around me.

I'd never have been up for something like this when I was thirteen. And a half. At that point, when it came to using my powers, I still had on the training wheels. What I'm attempting now is the equivalent of ditching the training wheels, along with the front wheel, and effectively riding a unicycle while blindfolded. Back then I'd have been terrified to drift down into so much nothingness. I would've been afraid of losing focus and, thanks to that fear, would likely have done so. I would have become trapped, suffering the same horrible death I warned Emma about. Except it would have been me instead of her, which would truly have sucked.

Just briefly, I hear the faint buzz that means Emma is trying to talk to me inside my head. Then it fades, and quickly I'm out of range, because I'm descending that far that fast. In no time at all, I'm completely on my own. If something goes wrong, no one can reach me. No one can help me.

On the other hand, no Emma Frost, so, y'know…bonus.

I continue to drift, like someone in free fall in a low-gravity environment. There is no end in sight. There is nothing in sight.

Okay. Definitely weird.

Suddenly I feel the area beneath my feet starting to "thin out." My secondary mutation, I guess, is informing me that my long, strange trip is nearly over.

I do a somersault so I can emerge head-first. Obviously I don't remember my birth, but if I did, I'd probably be reliving it right about now.

I come out into an environment filled with red light. Maybe it's a red-light district. Har de har—

Then I hit the floor.

Floor? This is a floor?

I don't know what the hell it is. This is like nothing I've ever seen. Not metal so much as…I'm not sure what. There are strange patterns on the floor, on the wall. Squares but with rounded edges. It almost reminds me of the shell of a tortoise. There's a dropoff to my left that seems to go on forever, spiraling away into darkness, and a pillar to my right that stretches up and back around itself. It all seems vaguely familiar, somehow…

Then I remember. It looks like footage I've seen taken with microscopic cameras. Film of the inside of human veins; that same kind of twisting and turning feeling, except that there's no blood. There's just me.

I suddenly feel like I'm some kind of microorganism. Is this not actually metal all around me, but something bio-organic? Am I inside some manner of living creature? I can't say that's a notion I'm too thrilled about, that I'm like a germ, inside of a host body. Especially since such intrusions don't generally end well for the germs.

There are long corridors stretching out in either direction. I arbitrarily pick left and start walking, trying to get a better idea of what the hell I was phasing through. It felt… wrong. It's not from this planet or any one I've been to. The molecular structure is…I hope it didn't do any permanent damage, passing through me…

Drop it, Kitty. Job to do. Keep it together.

I run my fingers along the wall as I go. It feels warm, even faintly pulsing. My first instinct may have been correct: bio-organic. Maybe I should count myself lucky it hasn't sent an alien version of white corpuscles to attack me.

Yet.

I hear voices. They sure sound like normal human voices, not alien ones. On the other hand, I've met aliens who sound more human than a lot of humans I know. So who knows for sure?

Peering out from around a corner, I see four guys armed with high-tech rifles. They look a lot like those rifles that Ord's goons were shooting off back at the penthouse. The same rifles that Scott said were boosted from S.H.I.E.L.D., even though Fury said he had no idea how they'd gotten into someone else's hands. I'm not sure if this thing is making more sense now, or less.

One of the men says, "Alpha Team has hostiles contained upstairs. No sign of breach, but we're on red just in case."

Crap. Crappity crappity crap. There's only one group of "hostiles" they can possibly be talking about.

And suddenly I'm thirteen and a half again, the only person running around free while the rest of the X-Men have been captured. I'm alone. Everything's resting on me.

Then I brush that aside. That was a long time ago. I've survived a hell of a lot and I'm still here and, oh right, I've also saved the rest of the team on any number of occasions. And if the "contained hostiles" means the rest of the X-Men, then it's up to me to find the truth about this place. Four guards? I've squared off with Juggernauts, not to mention alien monsters that would make James Cameron and Ridley Scott wet themselves. Bring it on.

That's when they say something that immediately grabs my attention:

"No one gets near the subject."

And when the guard says it, he looks in the direction of, and points toward, another hallway. One just off to my right. He means it as a casual gesture, but he's inadvertently guiding me right toward where I have to go.

It's a door. A big honking door, like you'd see in front of a bank vault. It's smooth, solid, with some sort of complex, alien-looking lock.

And inside that vault, there is apparently a "subject." Someone these bozos don't want any "hostiles" near. That means they've got something cooped up that would be of interest to the X-Men, and that's right in my wheelhouse.

I'm a little out of practice on my ninja training, but it's like falling off a bicycle or riding a log, whatever. You don't forget.

They're paying no attention, too caught up in their little conference to notice me. I run lightly down the hall toward the gigantic door.

Descending a hundred feet or more through solid what-ever-it-was has taken a lot out of me. Otherwise I would just phase through the door. But I need a few minutes to rest, and I'm not sure I have a few minutes. Besides, the door might be tricked out with some manner of booby trap; a disruptive field, perhaps, that could scramble even my molecules.

But the lock? Alien or no, there's not a lock I can't pop.

I ease my hand into the lock, and seconds later I disrupt the electronic flow of the inner circuitry. I hear the sound of bolts disengaging. The door swings wide on hinges that are a bit louder than I'd like, but I try not to worry about that.

I go to the door and gaze in. Everything's dark. There seems to be something huddling in there, but I can't quite make it out…a large, vague shape.

A voice bellows from behind me. "We have a hostile!"

They must have heard the sounds the door made. "Drop her! Drop her!" And they open fire.

Just as that happens, I hear a noise from inside the room, an insanely familiar sound. A clacking like metal plates snapping into place, one atop another very quickly.

I know this sound.

Knew this sound.

Know this sound.

I'm so startled by it, I almost forget to phase through the bullets. They pass through my chest...

And they klink off something behind me.

Something metal.

I turn around.

And my mind nearly shuts down. The only part of it that's still functioning is the part that's reminding me to remain intangible.

There, gleaming red in the reflected light, is Peter Rasputin.

Is Colossus.

He's nearly naked, clad only in red shorts. For a moment I think it's some sort of statue; they made a statue of Colossus for some reason, maybe as a memorial, even though that makes zero sense. They hate mutants. They call us "hostiles." Why would they make a statue of Colossus? But obviously they have, because it's standing right there in front of me, and sure, it's ridiculous, but it's the only explanation because Colossus is dead, everyone knows he's dead.

And then the statue's head swivels and looks at me. Right at me, with a kind of vague surprise, as if it thinks it should know me but doesn't.

The statue moves. It comes right at me, a barrage of bullets passing through me and striking it, bouncing off harmlessly. I always loved that an eternity ago, when I was thirteen and a half. Bullets would hit Wolverine, and he would stagger and stumble and then right himself and keep on going as his body healed, and he would boast about being unstoppable. Colossus...my Peter...he really was unstoppable. He would wade hip deep into any situation, and the bullets would just ricochet off him, occasionally even striking one of his attackers. He didn't make a big noise about it. He just went about his business, getting it done, not even bothering to acknowledge the stuff they threw at him. A walking statue, a man of few words. Outside, impenetrable. Inside, a big softy.

And I can see myself pouring out my underage heart to him, telling him what I feel for him. He is telling me sadly that it would not be right. We live in a world filled with people who turn trust into betrayal, who prey on the innocent. And here was this gentle giant of a Russian letting me down as easily as he could. And I grew up, and his life ended, and now literally not a day goes by that I don't think of him, imagine him alive, me holding him, me loving him and him me. Sometimes those imaginings seem so real that it's tempting to just release reality altogether and surrender myself to fantasy.

And that's apparently what's happened. Too much mutant hatred, too much discord, apparently it's all crashed down on me abruptly and without warning. (Okay, there was plenty of warning.) Because he's here, and he cannot be here, so obviously I must have checked out. Or maybe one of those bullets somehow didn't pass through me and lodged in my brain, and this is what they mean when they say your life passes before your eyes as you're dying.

Colossus is passing before my eyes.

Colossus is coming right at my eyes.

Colossus is passing through my eyes. Through my phasing body as the bullets continue to blow past me, and then he's behind me. I hear screaming, and weapons breaking, and more screaming, and bones crunching, and more screaming, and I still can't move from where I'm standing. My hand comes up of its own accord, rests on my heart. He's touched my heart, literally, as his upper body went through my chest.

Then I hear something hit the wall with an awful crunch, and a noise from a throat that sounds horrifyingly close to a death rattle.

It snaps me out of it, and I whisper, "Peter?"

He is in the process of shoving one of the guard's heads against the wall. Cracks are spreading out from the impact point. He's pushed this guy's head against the wall with such force that he's actually shattering the wall. God only knows what it's doing to the man's skull.

Their weapons lie scattered and broken all over the floor. One of the guards is running for his life.

Is the man Peter's pounding on still alive? He seems to be, barely.

"Stop, Peter!" I call.

Peter pulls him away from the wall, leaving blood smears behind. He lifts the soldier up as if the man weighs nothing, which—to Peter—is pretty much the case. He lifts the man over his head and throws him with such force that it's terrifying to see. The man collides with his fellow soldier, who's trying to flee the scene, and they both go down. They sprawl in a heap on the floor, both unconscious, and Peter advances on them, ready to do more damage even though they're helpless.

"Peter, stop!" I say again, this time more forcefully. I still don't understand why or how this is happening, but it is, and I have to deal with the here and now. "You'll kill them!"

He turns and looks right at me, and this time he seems to recognize me. The metal on his body dissolves, and the last doubt I had—my fear that this was some sort of robot—dissipates. It's Peter, standing there in the flesh.

"Katya?" he whispers. That's what he always called me, and my heart starts to truly beat for the first time in an age.

He sinks to his knees, as if he were praying. "Oh God." His voice is still low, as filled with incredulity as is my entire mind. He looks unfocused, confused, broken, and he reaches out for me, his hands on my hips, then around my back. His muscled arms are warm and alive. "Finally… God…am I…God, please…

"…am I finally dead?"

Maybe he is.

Maybe we both actually are. But if this is what dead is like, it beats the hell out of the life I've been living lately.

SIXTEEN

EMMA Frost forced herself to detach from the emotions roiling through her mind. In the past, before Scott entered her life, that would have been easy. Then her life and Scott's had become intertwined. She had let down her guard despite every instinct to the contrary, and now she actually had to force herself to mentally take a step back so she could assess the situation…something that was harder than it should have been because of her feelings for Scott, who was lying there injured. For half a heartbeat she allowed herself to wonder if her relationship with Scott was a liability, weakening rather than strengthening her. Then she pushed the notion away as unacceptable, and focused on the situation at hand.

Wolverine was down, unmoving. The Beast was snarling as he faced the armored figures. Clearly he wanted to attack, but knew he was targeted and would have been shot to pieces before he could make a move.

"On your knees, Cookie Monster," growled one of the soldiers, "or I swear to God I'll kill you."

The Beast visibly struggled, torn, ready to make a suicidal lunge. Then he appeared to think better of it and sank to his knees as instructed.

Abruptly Emma heard a female voice shouting, filled with outrage and alarm. *What is this?! Let me through!* The sheer fury radiating from the woman was enough to make the soldiers step to the side, allowing her through.

Emma's thoughts speared out at her. This was Kavita Rao: the enemy incarnate, the woman in the process of trying to destroy their lives. Emma planned to rip her memories right out of her gray matter and crush them like grapes, then savor the taste of the newly created wine.

But instead Emma felt her thoughts turned away, as effortlessly as a flitting moth.

The guard turned toward Rao. "This is a hostile zone, Doctor. Is your scrambler—?"

"It's on. Now move."

So Rao's mind was protected by the same device that shielded the soldiers. *They have no natural talents in a fight,* Emma thought angrily, *so they have to depend upon artificial means to defend themselves. Big guns, scramblers. They don't hate us because they're afraid of us. They hate us because they're jealous of us.*

Kavita Rao pushed past the soldiers and saw the X-Men clearly for the first time. Cyclops on the floor, the Beast on his knees with a huge gun pointed at his head to make sure he didn't move. Wolverine also lying on the floor, recovering from the bullet holes that had been pumped into him.

Rao turned to the soldiers, appalled. "You *fired* on them?"

"Man, the lady is sharp," Wolverine managed to say.

"Watch this one in particular," said the foremost of the guards, indicating Wolverine.

"Yeah...watch real *real* close," said Wolverine.

Stand down, Emma's voice sounded in his head.

Screw that. I can take these guys...

Not before bullets start flying, and you're the only one here with a healing factor. Hank was about to attack and I just talked him out of it; now you damned well stay put before I make you stay put. Clear?

A pause.

Wolverine...

Fine. Fine.

Having attended to one situation, however tenuously, Emma turned her attention to other matters. Indicating Cyclops, she said, "I need to get this man home."

Rao went to a cabinet on the wall. She pulled open the doors, revealing first-aid supplies. She removed bandages and what appeared to be a bottle of hydrogen peroxide. Pointing at the squad leader, she ordered, "One of you call in our med team."

The soldier didn't move. He just smirked. Obviously a dying mutant wasn't worth wasting a physician on.

"You realize I have the authority to fire you, right?" said Doctor Rao.

He glowered, and then went to an emergency phone on the wall. He picked it up and informed whoever was on the other end that a med team was required immediately.

Meanwhile Rao was unwrapping the gauze, preparing to apply it to Cyclops' wounds. "A Band-Aid's going to do sweet F.A., Doctor," said Emma.

"We have qualified surgeons not two buildings down…"

"And we have a *healer* at home," Emma countered.

"They're not going anywhere," the squad leader announced. "These people are trespassing in a top-security area. If they got themselves shot up, that's their own lookout. They should have known better—"

"We got *ourselves* shot up?" *Give me thirty seconds with them without their precious scramblers. I'll make sure they spend the rest of their lives in agony every time they take a piss.* "What do you think happened here? We threw ourselves on your bullets, which just happened to be floating there? You shot us when we were ready to leave."

"You broke in. You don't get to decide you're ready to leave."

And they'll only be able to move their bowels when they're standing near a telephone pole. Like the dogs they are.

Rao was kneeling next to Emma, cleaning Cyclops' wounds, bandaging them quickly and efficiently. Emma noticed the bud of the scrambler device in Rao's ear.

"I promise, I have no intention of hurting you," said Rao.

"Long as you've got that scrambler device in your left ear, I can't know *what* you intend."

Rao indicated one of Cyclops' still-bleeding wounds. "Put pressure on that." She glanced toward the Beast, who remained frozen in place, just as he had been when she first walked in. "Is Doctor McCoy all right? He—"

"He has a disease, if you recall." Emma pressed down on Cyclops' wound; the bleeding was slowing down. "An inexplicable aversion to being shot at."

"I never authorized this kind of force," said Rao. "I don't want anyone hurt. That's the whole point."

"Nothing but noble intentions, yes. You're a veritable Oppenheimer. What's next? Eliminating the gay gene?"

"Homosexuality doesn't represent a threat to human existence."

"We're clearly watching different televangelists," Emma said drily. "Not to mention different debates in the political arenas. At some point a candidate is going to run for president on a platform of forbidding gay mutants to marry, and they'll win in a landslide."

"I'd vote for him," said the squad leader.

"Shut up," said Rao.

Emma glanced around. "Where the hell is that med team? Are they even coming?"

"I'm sure they're on their way," said Rao. "As for your opinions, Miss Frost, I respect your concerns—"

"Yes, I can see the respect with which we're being treated. Careful you don't get any of this man's blood on you; you might catch what we have."

"—but the world needs this cure. Nothing you say or do is going to change that fact."

Now, said Emma, but silently and not to Rao.

Then a blue-furred hand clamped onto Rao's throat.

The Beast moved so quickly that he caught Kavita Rao completely off guard. One moment he had been crouched over, seemingly harmless, even bowed in terror. The next he was snarling in her face, teeth bared, yellow eyes glowing with fury and hatred. At that moment he wasn't recognizable as anything that could have once been a rational man.

Rao stared into the face of the Beast, and there was stark terror in her eyes.

The soldiers immediately leveled their massive guns. "Down! Put her down! Do it now!"

"Or what?" Emma said, thoroughly enjoying the show. "You'll open fire? Those weapons are built for shock and awe; you'll riddle her with bullets along with him."

The squad leader shifted his attention to Emma. "Fine. Then he lets her go or we kill you." And he swung his guns around to face Emma.

I'll kill 'em first, Wolverine's voice sounded in Emma's head.

Stay in reserve, Logan. I swear to you, you'll get your chance.

Aloud, she said haughtily to the squad leader, "Yes, by all means, you do that. Having nothing to lose, he'll then break her neck. And you get to explain to your superiors how a situation you could have handled peacefully escalated into the death of their star researcher."

"*Shut up,*" snarled the Beast. *"All of you!"*

He dragged Rao over to the table where the corpse of the young mutant lay right where it had been. "The world needs this cure, Kavita?" He yanked the thin sheet away from the female corpse on the table. She lay there naked and vulnerable, almost painful to look at. Rao tried to turn away, but the Beast grabbed her head from behind and forced her to look. "Did *she* need it? Did this girl need your cure?"

Her glasses askew, Kavita managed to say, "Hank...this girl was already dead. She killed herself..."

"Who else?" Beast said tightly. "I need to hear it from you, Kavita. Who else have you been cutting up?"

"I..." She adjusted her glasses. "I don't know what you mean."

"Did you think I wouldn't have the DNA on file, Doctor? The trace strands that I found in your sample?"

"What DNA?" Kavita genuinely sounded lost. "This girl's...?"

"Don't fence with me, Kavita, I'm not in the mood. You know whose DNA. An individual with transformative powers...who could switch from a mutant form to what you would call 'normal.' A good starting point for what you wanted to accomplish."

The guards were trying to angle around, find a shot that wouldn't endanger Rao. Beast's back was to them, but his ears were twitching. He effortlessly adjusted his position, keeping Rao in the line of fire.

Emma reached out with her mind. *Logan...you good to go?*

You know I am. What's the play?

They have those scramblers in their left ears. I would far prefer that they did not.

Not just a straight up slice-and-dice? You're not makin' it easy, Frost.

Too much of a challenge?

No. But there's three of them, one of me, and their guns are ready. I'm fast, but I could use a distraction. Especially if we wanna minimize bullets flying.

I'll see what I can do.

"Hank, I swear on my life—" Rao pleaded.

"Which is, at the moment, in my hands."

"—that I have no idea…" Her voice choked. It was a struggle to get out the rest. "…no idea what the hell you're talking about!"

To Emma, it almost sounded true. This woman was a scientist, not an actress.

Obviously, the Beast felt similarly. It drove him to a startling realization. "My God," he said, "you're a sham. You had help. Someone else was doing the heavy lifting on the research. Who was it, Kavita?" His voice escalated to a full-blown roar. "*Who are you covering for? Who's the real brains behind your precious cure? Who was the devil you struck your bargain with?*"

Kavita couldn't respond. Her mouth was open, but she was making little "urkh" noises and trying to shake her head.

Then Emma felt a gentle caress of fingers upon her hand. "Emma," Cyclops whispered, so softly that only she could hear him.

Her heart leaped with joy, but she kept her attention fixed on Beast and Rao. She didn't want to give any hint that Cyclops had regained consciousness.

Scott, darling. Don't try to talk, her thoughts sounded in his head.

The edges of his mouth twitched in an approximation of a smile. *You really got scared. I can feel it when you think at me. It's very sweet. Now...patch me in to the others.*

Very well. Logan...Hank...I have Scott for you on line two. Go ahead, Scott.

"Hank," Rao was saying desperately. "You know the only way to help further research is to work on the dead. I'm trying to create a world where this girl would never think of taking her own life. But since she already had—"

Hank, when I give the order, take Rao down to the floor. I want her out of the line of fire, friendly or otherwise.

Beast nodded. "I gotcha," he said aloud. "Good."

"What?" Rao blinked in confusion.

Logan...?

Just waiting on you, Slowpoke.

Cyclops opened his eyes. The ruby quartz shield of his visor glowed red. *Then let's show these Battlebot rejects who they're dealing with. GO!*

An optic blast ripped across the room, the air sizzling as it passed. It struck all three guards simultaneously, blasting them off their feet with enough concussive force to flatten a herd of elephants.

Beast shoved Rao down, landing on top of her, flattening her to the floor. His right foot accidentally hooked onto the corpse of the unknown mutant on the table and dragged it down with them.

The guards, filled with fear and terror, were at their most dangerous, likely to just start shooting wild. With all those bullets flying, they would inevitably hit *something*. Each other. Emma. Cyclops. The Beast or Rao, even though he was shielding her with his body.

Wolverine immediately took care of that possibility.

He leaped upon the guards, his claws flashing. He sliced through their guns, shattering the mechanisms. Bullet shells tumbled out of ammunition casings without being fired.

But Wolverine knew the guards might have other weapons on them. He had no intention of allowing those weapons to be used.

Logan, Scott's voice sounded in his head, *you need to...*

Emma already gave me my marching orders. They get the Van Gogh treatment.

And he thrust forward with his claws.

The soldiers' ears were covered with white-noise units to protect their hearing from the deafening clattering of gunfire. Wolverine didn't waste time being delicate. He slashed, and his claws sliced away not only the white-noise units over the men's ears, but also the ears themselves. The guards screamed, nearly in unison, as blood began to pour down the sides of their heads. Their ears lay on the floor, nothing more than small pieces of freshly severed meat.

"And that would be the end of the scramblers," said Emma calmly as the guards staggered, grasping at the sides of their heads, moaning in anguish. "Well, here's some good news: *You feel no pain.* Now…pick up your ears…don't get them mixed up, because that could hamper getting them reattached."

They did as she bade, peeling their respective ears off the floor and placing them carefully in pouches on their uniforms.

The Beast got to his feet, pushing the corpse of the young, dead mutant girl onto Rao, who squirmed under the weight. Emma considered that extremely rude. She also thought it appropriate.

"Does the five-second rule apply to body parts?" asked Wolverine.

"Yes," said Emma. "Now, stand at attention."

The guards snapped upright, staring straight ahead.

Emma studied them dispassionately. She considered the things she had previously contemplated doing to them, and decided she would dial it down ever so slightly. But not too much. "You will go straight to a hospital. You will remember nothing of this place. And…" She provided a dramatic pause, allowing them to contemplate their fates.

…every time you hear the words 'parsley,' 'intractable,' or 'longitude,' you will vomit uncontrollably for forty-eight hours. You may go now."

They pivoted briskly on their heels and headed out the door.

"Nice work, X-Men," said Cyclops. He saw the Beast staring at him with a raised eyebrow, nodding ever so slightly toward Emma. Cyclops lowered his voice. "My girlfriend is very weird," he acknowledged.

"I'm not about to argue that point," said Beast. "So what do we do now?"

Wolverine spoke up. "Emma takes Scott back to the school, Hank and me find Kitty, and then we burn this place to the ground."

"First off, Scott and I give the orders, Logan," Emma said. "Second, good plan."

"It won't help." Rao had pushed the body of the dead girl off herself. Having gotten to her feet, she was busy straightening her clothing. "I've already given samples and all my data to hundreds of teams around the world. 'Miracle' can't be crushed now. Not even by you."

A slow smile spread across Wolverine's face. "Nice bluff. But I call. Do you really think we're gonna just decide it's not worth our time to trash this place because your cure's already gone viral?"

"Do what you want," she said, her voice flat. "All I'm telling you is that it's a waste of your time."

"Yes, Kavita, that's what you're *telling* us," Beast spoke up. "On the other hand, all you have to do is remove that little device in your ear and allow Emma to verify what you're thinking as opposed to what you're saying. So if it wouldn't be too much trouble—"

"You're many things, Doctor McCoy," she said formally, "but I know you are not stupid. Kindly do the courtesy of crediting me with equal intelligence. I saw what she just did to those men. The moment I leave my brain open to her, she's going to fry it like an egg. I won't have any recollection of my work on 'Miracle.' I'll be lucky if I remember how to tie shoelaces. Isn't that right, Miss Frost?" and she looked toward Emma.

Emma was standing there with a stunned look on her face. "Incredible," she was saying. Her attention seemed very far away, as if she were carrying on another conversation in her head. Then she seemed to notice the others looking at her in confusion. Quickly she gathered herself and said distantly, "That is a... distinct possibility, to be candid. On the other hand, perhaps I won't. Depends upon my mood."

"Here's a nutty thought," said Wolverine, raising his claws toward Rao. "How about I give you a choice...which is more than the government is going to give mutants, sooner or later, when it comes to your cure. Either yank that thing out of your ear and take your chances, or I come over there and take it out myself, which ain't gonna be fun for either of us. Well...maybe for me."

Rao gulped deeply. Her hand didn't move. She seemed too paralyzed to do anything. Wolverine took a step toward her...

And the far wall caved in.

Ord of the Breakworld crashed through, roaring with fury, sending wall, machinery and everything else in his way scattering in all directions. Wolverine and Beast leaped clear. Cyclops dove and hit the ground. Debris flew harmlessly over his head, but the impact exacerbated his wounds. Splotches of blood appeared on the bandages wrapped around his torso.

Grinning in triumph, Ord said, "And to think *I* went looking for *you*."

"There are doors, you know," said Rao. She had managed to regain her composure. "Right there, on either end of the room. Would it have killed you to use one of them? Was your dramatic entrance really necessary?"

Emma stepped between Rao and Ord, hatred on her face. Before their eyes, she transformed into her diamond form. Ord did not appear the slightest bit impressed. "How heroic to put yourself between me and a woman you loathe. I would not have expected that measure of generosity from a stone-cold creature such as you. If it's of any comfort, I have neither interest nor desire in killing Doctor Rao. You, on the other hand…" He pulled out his circular, bladed weapon. "Your diamond form is quite scintillating. But there is no substance on Earth this blade cannot cut through."

Upon hearing that, Emma promptly pulled Rao around in front of her, using her as a human shield.

"Good to know," Emma said.

THE Beast was starting to put it all together. As he'd said before, Kavita had obviously had outside help in creating the cure…and now Ord seemed not to want to harm her. She seemed to mean something to him, and Beast suspected it wasn't love between them.

He and Wolverine approached Ord from different sides, trying to get into position for a perfect attack. Then Emma shoved Kavita Rao straight at Ord. He knocked Rao aside, sending her crashing into a counter. She banged her head against a cabinet and her glasses went flying. Beast was reasonably sure it must have hurt like hell.

Oddly enough, he couldn't find any measure of pity for her.

Wolverine had his claws out. He had positioned himself in front of Cyclops, crouched and ready.

Beast waited for Emma to link in, coordinate their attack. But she was uncharacteristically silent, as if her mind were elsewhere. "Plan?" he said briskly to the snarling, clawed mutant to his left.

Wolverine was his characteristic, succinct self. "Man's got eyeballs."

"And," Emma added, her voice still sounding distracted, "if he's a man by our definition, that's not the only soft target…"

Wolverine and the Beast froze. They'd been moving toward Ord, readying for their assault, and then they stopped right where they were.

Ord's horrible smile spread across his face. "Too scared for stratagems, X-Men? Then maybe it's time we finished this."

———————— 🖋 ————————

All the times I envisioned Peter naked, or at least nearly naked, in front of me…the two of us alone…

It was never like this.

We're sitting about ten feet away from each other. The room is bathed in red, with alien pillars and curves all around us. Somehow it's thematically appropriate. I feel like I'm having an out-of-Earth experience. Like I've left my body somehow and been transported into an alternate world where Peter is perfectly fine. I've switched bodies somehow with the Kitty Pryde who's supposed to be here, and she's off in my world where Peter is dead, and now she has to live with a huge hole in her heart. And I'm here with him, and of course that doesn't make sense.

I know none of it is true. I'm here. He's here. He's here and he's not here, all at the same time, and I haven't traveled to another universe. Instead different universes are collapsing in upon me, and I don't know what to say and I don't know what to do. And all that time he's just sitting there, sitting with his back rigid, his hands resting on his knees, like an oversized Russian schoolboy.

He's the schoolboy and I'm the teacher, and he's waiting for me to say something. So I say the first thing that comes into my mind.

SEVENTEEN

"I'M gonna need a minute here."

Peter stared at her.

"Before I can get us out, I'm gonna need to rest," she went on. "It's hard getting through this metal, and taking you along...it's gonna be a little..."

"You look different."

They were the first words he'd spoken since he'd collapsed in front of her, on his knees, asking if he were finally dead. She had assured him that he wasn't, and helped him to the seated position, which he had maintained from that moment to this. His brain seemed to be desperately striving to catch up with the events unfolding around him.

"Well...yeah," said Kitty. "I look different because I am. Different."

He nodded slowly, processing that. "Has it been very long, then?"

Slowly she got to her feet, her body a torrent of emotions colliding with each other. Peter watched, unmoving, with that same vaguely confused look. She was fighting to keep herself together. "I'm sorry. You have to know that if you're a clone or a robot or, yeah, a ghost, or an alternate-universe thingie, I can deal with that."

"That's good to know."

"Glad you approve," and then her voice began to rise, the obvious fear of having her impossible, fantastic dream granted, her precious Peter Rasputin returned to her, only to see it crash and burn…it was starting to overwhelm her and she couldn't stand it. "But if you are some shape-shifter or illusionist who's just watching me twist, I will kill you. I will kill you with…" She hesitated, then said at random, "…an axe. I will kill you with an axe, so right away, just *prove* it. Say something. Show me something. Show me something I can't—"

"Katya," he began to say gently.

"*You died!*" There was no point in trying to interrupt her now; she was on a roll. "Peter Rasputin died, and I know this because I carried his ashes to Russia and scattered them myself!"

For the first time, that impassivity in his face, that detached air, melted. There was no stammered denial, no attempt to present a clean, tidy explanation for the impossibility of his return. Nothing at all except a genuinely startled look. Which was exactly what one would have expected from such a self-effacing individual as Peter Rasputin, the humble farm boy. "You did?" he said. When she nodded, he looked down at his feet as if he were chagrined. Then he looked back up at her. "Thank you."

She wanted to laugh and cry all at the same time. It was such an understated reply: nonsensical, yet it made perfect sense. It was quintessential Peter. No mere shape-shifter could have come up with a response like that. She put a hand to her head to steady herself, turning her back to him because she didn't want him to see her like this. "I'm so sorry. You need my help, and I'm...I feel so weak."

He was behind her then, resting a hand on her shoulder. Even in his human form, that single hand would have had enough power to break her neck had he been so disposed. Instead it was as gentle as a mother stroking the face of her newborn child. "They switched my body with someone else, I think. Revived me and...and brought me here. I don't know whose ashes..." He stopped. "I am not a trick."

"I know." She turned to face him. "I mean, I think that I...I know."

He looked down at her and there was such exhaustion in his eyes. They were the eyes of a man who had been through nine kinds of hell and could scarcely believe it was over. She reached up to him and he took her hand, wrapping his fingers around it. It seemed tiny in his grasp. "I can feel your hand, and I am certain...I am also not a ghost."

It took her a moment to compose herself. She closed her eyes, and then opened them. "Okay, so... rescue." She glanced around, trying to look past the bodies of the guards that were sprawled on the floor. They weren't moving, and she wasn't even sure if they were breathing. She thought about waking them up and questioning them. But if Peter had inflicted upon them damage too severe for them to have survived— if he had, in fact, killed them—then she quite simply did not want to know about it.

Kitty knew she could float upward through the metal, but if there was an alternative, then she definitely wanted to pursue it. "Do you know any other way out besides up? I don't think these guys came down through a hundred feet of metal, do you?"

"No."

"'No' you don't think they came through the metal, or—?"

"No," he clarified, "I do not know any other way up. I only know the room. Always dark inside. Cold. They kept me strong, healthy...I pounded the walls every day, every minute, for years...was it years?"

"I...don't know for sure how long, because I have

no idea how long you've been…you know…not dead."
She was anxious to move away from this line of conversation. "In this…this cold room…what did they—?"

"Tests," he said hollowly. "They did tests. I would lie in darkness, in that…that place you found me. And from time to time—I want to say every few days, but it is impossible to know, it could have been weeks, it could have been every day—the gas would come. It was always when I was asleep…"

"Because when you're in your armored form, you don't need to breathe."

He nodded. "So I would try not to sleep. But it was impossible. Sooner or later, exhaustion would overtake me. And when I would awaken still in darkness, I would actually be grateful. Can you imagine such a thing? Grateful to awaken in darkness, in a cage. But that was better than waking up in the room with the table…"

"Table?"

He nodded. "Yes. A sort of operating table. It had four clamps, two for the arms and two for the legs. I would awaken strapped down, and there were machines all around. Machines with blades of all kinds and other devices designed to tear away at me. I would wake on that table, and they would cut me, inject…things…"

Kitty fought to remain focused on his words, trying not to cry at the thought of what he had been put through, what he had endured. If Peter was aware of the turmoil going through her mind, he didn't show it. Trying to stick to business, she said, "Did you ever see their faces?" If he did have a description…if it was someone she actually recognized…she knew she'd be tempted to go kill the bastard herself.

He shook his head. "All I saw were their masks." Before the look of disappointment appeared on her face, however, he continued, "And *him.* The one who brought me back. One who is not of this world. He would look down upon me, his face a sickly pale green, and he would say things like, 'Congratulations, Peter Rasputin. You were dead, and I have brought you back…to make certain you die again after we are done with you.'" He saw the look on her face. "Katya, is something wrong—?"

"Ord," she said. Her face conveyed pure focused fury.

"What?"

"Ord. His name is Ord. It has to be him. It's too much of a coincidence not to be. The description matches, plus that sounds like the kind of thing he'd say."

"You know him?"

"It's not like we're best buds or anything. We fought him." In quick, broad strokes she laid out the circumstances under which they had met Ord. Her mind was whirling. "I don't know what to think.

He…what you're saying is he brought you back to life somehow. Which I should be more grateful for than anything in my life, ever. And then he spends God-knows-how-long torturing you. So, y'know, kind of hard not to want to beat him to death. I don't know which way to—"

"Beating to death," said Peter. "Yes. That."

The only time she'd seen his face harder was when it was covered with armor. For an instant the seething hatred in his voice made her doubt, just slightly, that he was who he said he was. But then that doubt vanished. If she'd been through what he had, she knew she'd want a very personal kind of revenge, too.

"Okay, then," she said. She wasn't going to be getting any more rested. Remaining where they were at this point qualified as delaying the inevitable. "Let's do this thing. Come here."

He placed his arm around her. It took her breath away. He felt so warm, so alive. *Focus, Kitty, focus.* It wouldn't do either of them any good if she got so distracted by his touch that she left his corpse behind, fused to the wall.

Seconds later they were drifting upward. Whereas Emma Frost had been jumpy and uncertain, nearly getting herself killed while passing through the simple wall of a building, Peter was the picture of stoicism. *Probably perfected it during those long Russian winters.*

Up she went, and up, and then the blackness was complete around her. But her closeness to Peter, the fact that she was bringing him back to the life he'd lost, filled her with an internal radiance.

The first time she had traveled through the expanse below the floor of Benetech, the trip had seemed endless. This time, though, it felt much faster, perhaps because she had a clear idea of the journey's termination point. Finally she reached the top. Like ghosts, the two of them emerged from the floor and "landed" gently.

Lockheed the dragon was there, right where she'd left him. He looked from Kitty to Peter and didn't react in the slightest, as if he saw a dead guy emerging from the floor every day. He snorted with what could be termed, at best, mild interest, and then settled his head back down on his front claws. He yawned once, lazily, and then closed his eyes.

Kitty sagged against Peter. "Are you all right, Katya?" he asked.

"Sorry. This much phasing, especially through whatever weird-ass material that is...it's just taking it out of me a little bit. Don't worry, I'll be—"

There you are.

She shuddered and mentally recoiled. Emma Frost was in her head.

No one invited you, Kitty sent back sharply.

We were beginning to get worried. Although in my

case, *"worried"* is hardly the correct—

Then Emma realized who was standing next to Kitty. Her mental astonishment brought Kitty some degree of smug satisfaction.

Incredible.

Kitty thought she heard a vague echo, as if Emma had both thought the word and spoken it aloud simultaneously.

Yeah. Pretty impressive, huh? And it's him, I'm sure of it.

I know; I just scanned his mind. We knew he was here, but we all just assumed that he—

That brought Kitty to a halt. *You knew? You knew he was here? How the hell long did you know—?*

Henry discovered his DNA traces in the cure. We wanted to recover his corpse. We weren't expecting that he was alive.

Rage bubbled within Kitty. *How the hell could you* not *tell me?! How could you possibly keep me out of the loop, knowing how I feel about him—!*

We did it exactly because we know how you feel. We needed you to be dispassionate and focused.

You lied to me!

Yes. We did. And when you're a leader, you'll keep your people on a need-to-know basis too, so get the hell over it and prove you can *focus when required. Or are you upset because you missed out on a second chance to spread his ashes?*

No…no, of course not. But you should have—
Damnation.

Kitty was irritated. *Now what the hell did I do—?*

Not everything is about you, Miss Pryde. It's Ord. He's here. He just bashed in a wall, which isn't so bad since the color scheme was simply ghastly.

He kept Peter prisoner all this time. Tortured him.

Then I think it only fair that Peter have an opportunity to repay him for his attentions.

Let him know.

I have, said Emma. *I'm in his mind as well. I just informed him.*

Really? I can't hear his thoughts. Usually when—

That's my doing, Emma told her. *There's irony in my saying this, I know, but trust me. The relentless string of profanities running through his mind right now is nothing you want to be exposed to. Might harm your perceptions of the big Russian teddy bear you're nursing.*

"We need to get me up there. As quickly as possible." It was Peter who had spoken, but it was Colossus who faced Kitty now. He had armored up, his body turned to solid metal. His pupils had vanished, as they always did when he took this form. It had never bothered her much before, but now he looked like a soulless thing eager for vengeance. She knew Peter Rasputin was buried somewhere inside that impenetrable shell. But until he managed to confront his tormentor, he would be nothing other than Colossus.

The mental exchange between them and Emma, if spoken aloud, would have taken several minutes. As it was, it only took seconds. *Speed is imperative,* Emma informed them. *This is about to escalate. Get up here immediately.*

I don't even know where you are. It may take me a few minutes to find you—

No point in wasting time. I can draw you right to us. But you'll have to effectively turn your mind over to me. It will require a deeper access than I normally take. The woman you think *I am would do it without your permission. Instead, I'm asking it.*

Because you know what I'm going to say.

I'm telepathic, Katherine, not a seer. Tell me what you want.

She looked at Colossus. "Why are we simply standing here," he said, "when Ord is—"

"Come here." It wasn't going to be easy; she was still exhausted from passing through the wall under the subbasement. At least the floors above them were made of nice, normal metal. *Okay, Emma...I'm giving you an all-access backstage pass. But don't you dare—*

And suddenly her mind was no longer her own. Her thoughts were still present, but her body was nothing more than a puppet on someone else's string. She drifted upward and phased through the ceiling, without conscious volition. She had no idea where she was going, yet somehow she knew: Kitty was being drawn inevitably toward where the X-Men were about to square off with Ord.

Then, deep in the recesses of her mind, she came to a horrible realization. Emma Frost held her life in her hands. Emma could easily, against Kitty's will, turn off her phasing power at any time. She and Peter would die instantly, and no one would ever know why. When, or if, what was left of their bodies was found, it would be assumed that her powers had malfunctioned somehow. No one—certainly not Cyclops—would think to turn the spotlight of suspicion on Emma Frost.

I would never do something like that, Emma said. *Not as long as I consider you to be of use.*

Kitty didn't find that particularly reassuring.

She drifted upward so quickly that the trip was a blur. And then, just when she thought she might lose herself forever in her own head, she floated up into a room filled with evidence of recent carnage.

"Man's got eyeballs," she heard Wolverine saying, and Emma said something in return about other soft body areas that could be assaulted. *Guiding me while facing off against Ord. God, the woman can multitask,* Kitty grudgingly admitted to herself.

Slowly Emma extracted her mind from Kitty's, and suddenly Kitty felt dizzy. The combination of all the phasing and Emma's mental control had taken its toll. It was all Kitty could do to keep herself together long enough to finish materializing herself and Colossus, directly behind Ord.

Beast, Wolverine and Emma stood facing him, and suddenly they saw who had just emerged from the floor. The Beast and Wolverine were gaping, stunned. Even Emma, who had learned of Peter's existence moments earlier, looked amazed, as if his survival hadn't seemed real until he was right in front of her.

Ord completely misinterpreted their reactions. "Too scared for stratagems, X-Men? Then maybe it's time we finished this."

Wolverine found his voice before the Beast and Emma did, which was impressive considering that of the three of them, he was the most out of the loop.

"Okay," he said. "Yeah. Why don't we do that?"

Ord was slowly beginning to figure out that something was wrong. "What are you all looking—?" His voice trailed off. He closed his eyes. "Oh no. Is that dragon thing behind me?"

He received his answer a split second later as Colossus stepped forward and drove a steel-plated fist into the small of Ord's back. A loud "clang" resounded throughout the room.

Ord staggered, let out a startled cry of pain, and turned to face his assailant. There was utter incredulity on his face. *"You!"* he bellowed.

Colossus advanced on Ord. Nothing else existed in the world right then.

Ord's armored fist whipped around and hit Colossus squarely in the face. Colossus staggered. Ord struck again and again, delivering a withering barrage of blows as Colossus fought to stay on his feet. "It matters nothing that you've escaped. Do you think because you are made of mere steel that you can stand against me?"

He slashed forward with his lethal blade. Incredibly, considering his size, Colossus sidestepped it. Then he thrust forward and snagged Ord's left hand, which was holding the blade, immobilizing it. Ord tried to drive a punch into Colossus' gut, but Colossus caught his hand. Ord tried to pull away, but for a split-second he was off-balance.

Colossus snarled, "I am not made of steel," as he yanked Ord off his feet, twisted, and slammed the alien onto his back. The impact was so violent it created a crater beneath Ord, cracks ribboning across the floor like a spider's web. "Rage," continued Colossus, and he pivoted quickly, anchoring himself in place as Ord hit the floor again, groaning softly.

"I...am made..." and Colossus sent Ord flying across the room. Beast and Wolverine dove to either side as Ord crashed into a table full of lab equipment that had somehow, miraculously—until then—managed to stay intact. Now it went down under Ord's falling body and, before Ord could stand up, Colossus brought both his powerful fists down upon Ord. "...of *rage!*"

When he struck, the blow reverberated throughout the building.

And still Ord was trying to get back up. But Colossus kept pounding away, until his enemy stopped moving.

He looked to his teammates then, expectantly.

"Finish it, Pete," was all Wolverine had to say.

Colossus drew his fist back, and then Kitty said softly, "Peter…"

He turned to her.

Still on the ground, exhausted, she managed to hold his gaze as she said, barely above a whisper, "I've no right…to tell you not to…not after what he put you through. But…"

She couldn't finish the sentence. She didn't have to.

Colossus stared at her, and then at his fists, and at that moment Kitty couldn't say what he was going to do.

And then a familiar voice growled, "Sorry…you ain't gonna win this day."

Nick Fury, the head of S.H.I.E.L.D., entered the room, stepping over the debris that had fallen everywhere. He was accompanied by two dozen S.H.I.E.L.D. agents, all of them armed with vicious-looking guns aimed squarely at the X-Men. They spread out, keeping the mutants firmly in their sights. They weren't even bothering to try to avoid Doctor Rao; she was directly in their line of fire and not a single one of them appeared to give a damn.

Kitty saw that Fury was the only one in the lab who wasn't holding a gun. No…not the only one. A woman standing next to him also had her hands empty. She had green hair, sunglasses even though it was nighttime, and was the only one not clad in a S.H.I.E.L.D. uniform.

Emma, Kitty thought fiercely, wondering whether Frost would pick her up. *Can you…?*

Try to take over Fury's mind, make him issue orders that would send everyone home? No. He has one of those scramblers. They all do.

Jesus. Are they buying them by the carload?

It wouldn't matter even if I could grab hold of his mind. Fury's too sharp for that. His people would know the game plan, and if Fury said or did anything that deviated in the slightest from what they were supposed to do, his people would know and start opening fire.

Kitty was confused. *But if they start shooting, they'll hit Rao…*

I don't think they care about her.

Okay, but then why—?

"Back away from him, Tin Man," said Nick Fury, interrupting the conversation between Emma and Kitty, all of which had transpired at the speed of thought.

"Or—?" The humble, deferential tone that was Colossus' hallmark was gone. Instead he stood there defiant, unafraid.

Fury made a casual gesture toward the array of firepower directed at them. "These babies have the latest in armor-piercing technology. And if it just bounces off you, well, that's a lot of friendly fire to gamble everyone's lives on."

"Your people would be vulnerable to 'friendly fire' as well," said Colossus.

"Yeah, but they're willing to take that risk. You willing to risk your pals? Your call, big man."

Time hung frozen for a moment, and then Colossus, with a snarl of frustration, stepped away from Ord. He walked over to Kitty and crouched next to her protectively, his armor retracting to be replaced by human skin. His glower, however, remained.

A S.H.I.E.L.D. agent came forward and squatted next to Ord, who had just lapsed into unconsciousness. The agent started checking him over.

"Cyclops nearly got Swiss-cheesed by this place's goon squad," said Wolverine, "but all you guys care about is making sure the bad guy is okay?"

"We're doing our job, Logan," said Fury.

"So were we. Saving people's butts."

"No. This isn't your job. This is your hobby. And it seems like the only butts you're saving here are your own."

Cyclops had managed to bring himself upright. "There's some truth to that," he said, "but no one else was looking out for us, were they?"

Fury didn't respond.

"You still ain't told us why you're busy patching this guy up," Wolverine said, indicating Ord. "You worried he's gonna bleed out while you're bringing him to Gitmo or the Negative Zone or wherever you stash super-powered alien criminals?"

"He ain't a criminal, and he's not going to the lockup."

"What the hell are you talking about?"

"He's not a criminal," said Fury, "because our laws don't apply to him. He's an ambassador. He's got diplomatic immunity."

EIGHTEEN

EDDIE stared at his hands as if they belonged to someone else. The Stepford Cuckoos had departed the infirmary, declaring that they had done all they could and were now off to spread the word of Wing's mishap. This, they contended, qualified as "gossip" and so they were socially obligated to inform others.

Hisako had tried to argue them out of it, but the Cuckoos had said in unison, "*This is the equivalent of a casualty./ Out of respect for the fallen, word should be spread and tributes prepared.*" Hisako realized she had no answer for that, and the Cuckoos went on their way.

Meanwhile the "fallen" hadn't moved so much as a millimeter since he'd realized what had happened to him. Hisako, worried, gazed into his eyes. He didn't look back at her; instead he looked right through her. She said softly, "Eddie? You in there?"

"This isn't my body," he whispered. "My body can fly. This one can't. This isn't my body…"

"Eddie," and Hisako started to put her hand on his arm.

But he shook her touch away. She supposed that on one level, that was a good thing. At least he hadn't totally withdrawn into himself. Now they just had to—

Edward turned to Elixir. "Put it back," he said.

Elixir's golden face was puzzled. "Excuse me—?"

"Put it back. My power. You're a healer. Heal me."

"I can't," said Elixir. "I can only heal something that's broken, something that's…wrong."

"*This* is wrong," Eddie said vehemently, his voice rising. The first signs of genuine panic were beginning to set in. "This isn't who I am."

"Who you are is a normal person."

"Flying *is* normal for me! *That's* my normal!"

"This isn't a negotiation, Edward," said Elixir. "I'm not trying to be difficult or obstructionist. This isn't something you can find a loophole for, and it's not like I woke up this morning and said, 'Who can I be a total jerk to today? Hmmm. I'll pick Wing.' The fact is, you're not sick. I can't heal someone who isn't sick."

"An alien goon sticking me with some needles and taking away my power…that's the sick thing!"

"I don't disagree, but—"

"Then fix me! *Fix me!*"

"Eddie." Hisako didn't try to touch him this time.

But she stood between him and Elixir, trying to get his attention, speaking in soft, soothing tones.

To her shock, Eddie shoved Hisako to one side so violently that it knocked her to the floor. Then he was on Elixir, grabbing him by the front of the shirt, shaking him. *"Fix me, dammit! Fix me!"*

Elixir composed himself and grabbed Eddie by both wrists. "I know how bodies are put together," he said calmly, "which means I can do things like this." Keeping a firm grasp on Eddie's wrists, he twisted down and around. The maneuver turned Eddie's muscles against themselves, breaking his grip effortlessly. "Now I need you to—"

Edward drove his foot into Elixir's crotch.

Elixir let out a pained shriek and collapsed. Eddie stepped over the boy, his body shaking. "I can't live like this. *I can't live like this!*" And with that pronouncement, he darted through the door and out of the room.

Hisako jumped over Elixir to follow Eddie. Then she stopped and said in a hurried, flustered tone to Elixir, "Are you okay?"

Elixir grunted, which was about as close as he was going to come to a coherent response.

"Okay, well…good," and she bolted down the hallway after Eddie.

He was a short ways ahead of her, pounding down the hallway, and he kept shouting over and over, *"I can't live like this!"* Hisako was terrified, because there was no doubt in her mind that he absolutely meant it. It was as literal a call for help as she'd ever heard, and she was certain that if she didn't manage to get to him in time, he was going to act on his words. The old line flashed through her head: *Suicide is a permanent solution to a temporary problem.* But there was nothing temporary here. Eddie would never have his power again, and that problem was never going to go away. So he was going to make himself go away first.

"Eddie, wait! Wait!"

But he ignored her cries. Instead, before she could get near him, he made a sharp left turn and started running up the nearest stairs. *"Get away from me, Hisako!"* he howled. He disappeared up the stairs, running so fast that he was out of sight before she could even start climbing.

Then she heard a loud *thud* followed immediately by an "oooof." A series of repeated thumps quickly followed, as if a sack of potatoes—or perhaps a body—were tumbling down the stairs.

She sprinted up the stairs, taking them two at a time, and found Eddie stretched out on the landing halfway up. He was stunned, blinking, as if unsure where he was. Standing at the top of the stairs was an astounded Santo Vaccarro, otherwise known as Rockslide. The towering mutant had a body that, appropriately enough considering his code name, was covered with a rock-like hide. He stared down at the insensate Eddie in confusion.

"What's *his* problem?" Rockslide asked, his voice sounding like boulders crunching together.

"He lost his powers," she said as she knelt next to Eddie, looking down in concern.

"Powers of what? Observation? Idiot ran right into me."

"No, Santo. His power of flight. He's normal now."

"Normal?" Rockslide gave Eddie a contemptuous look. "Normal depends on your environment, doesn't it? We're in a school for mutants. *I'm* normal. *You're* normal. *He's* a freak."

"Shut up, Santo," she said angrily.

"Fine. Whatever." Rockslide shrugged indifferently and walked away, leaving Hisako cradling the still-groggy Edward.

"Eddie, are you okay?"

"Huh?" was all he managed to say.

She pulled him to his feet and, not knowing where else to go, brought him back to the infirmary. Elixir was right where she'd left him, on the floor, his hands covering his crotch. He was retching a bit and was still trying to pull himself together when he saw her enter with Eddie. Eddie offered no resistance as she laid him down on the table.

Elixir said nothing, probably not trusting himself to speak. She turned to face him and said tentatively, "Are you okay, Josh? Are you, y'know...healing it?"

"Nooo, I can't heal myself. This is where a guy's hand just automatically goes when he gets kicked in the nuts."

"Oh. Sorry."

Elixir nodded toward Eddie. "What happened to him?"

"Ran headlong into Rockslide."

"Good."

"He may have concussed himself."

"Even better."

"Come on, Josh, give him a break."

"I'd love to," Elixir said crankily, "but I'd probably just have to turn around and heal it again." He had managed to stand and was now leaning against the wall, breathing steadily in order to compose himself.

"He got a huge shock and he almost died. It's not his fault."

"Well, it's sure as hell not mine, either. He might be dead if it weren't for me."

"I know that, and on some level he knows that, too. He just needs time to...I don't know...adjust."

Eddie lay on the table, staring up at the ceiling. It was as if the impact from careening into Rockslide had knocked all the fight out of him. Hisako went over to Elixir and gestured with her head that they should step outside. With a weary sigh, and a very tentative stride, he followed her out into the hallway. Softly enough to make sure that Eddie couldn't hear her, she said, "*Is* there any chance that you could restore him to what he was?"

He looked genuinely regretful. "Believe me, I'd love to."

"But how do you know for sure? I mean, you don't even know how this drug works."

"I actually kind of do. When I heal someone, I don't just, y'know, 'fix' them. I get a sense of how their body works, all the chemical processes. It's not deliberate; it just comes with the territory." He paused, looking like he was trying to work out things in his head before going on. "The best I can explain it is that when mutants like you or me reach a certain age, something in the DNA triggers and the mutation presents itself. This thing...I think it may have reversed the trigger. Put the bullet back in the chamber."

"I'm not entirely sure I'm following."

He rubbed the bridge of his nose. "Okay, look... mutant powers typically show up when we hit adolescence, right? Because when adolescence happens, certain chemicals are released and cause changes in our bodies. Usually it's, y'know...body hair or breasts..."

"Not so much with the latter in my case," she said ruefully, "but I get it."

"Okay, but…it's not the hormones themselves that cause it. It's the actual release, like a starter's gun being fired, that kicks it off and causes the powers to manifest. This 'cure' that the alien shot into him overwrote that and suppressed the triggering of the gene."

"So…" She started to get excited. "So you're saying that his powers are still there?"

"Maybe."

"So why don't the hormones that are still in his body cause them to—?" Then she realized. "Because they're already present."

"Exactly. We can't replicate the first release of the hormones. Not without a time machine or a means of devolving him."

"Not right now we can't," said Hisako, determined not to give up. "But maybe if you study it with Doctor McCoy—"

"With who—? Oh. Right. Sorry," he looked embarrassed. "My first reflex when I hear that name is to think of the guy from *Star Trek*."

She looked at him blankly. "The only doctor I know from *Star Trek* is Doctor Spock."

"No, he's…" He waved it off. "Forget it. The point is, even if it's possible, it's a long way from definite. Until then, he's going to be stuck this way. He's going to have to learn to live with this."

Hisako looked at Eddie's forlorn expression, staring straight ahead into nothingness. A bruise was starting to swell on his forehead.

"Let's just hope that's an option," she said. "We'll have to see what the X-Men say when they get back."

NINETEEN

THE first word out of Wolverine's mouth was "Diplomatic." The last word was "immunity." In between those two words, however, a lengthy, florid string of profanity tumbled out of his mouth.

Colossus covered Kitty's ears.

When Wolverine's tirade finally ended, Fury said coolly, "You heard me, Tiny. And having heard, you walk away."

Fury was conceivably the only person in the world who could address Wolverine as "Tiny" and live. But Wolverine remained in a feral crouch, his arms drawn back, ready to leap to the attack.

"Walk away?" said Emma. "Not bloody likely."

"Play me straight, Fury," said Wolverine. "This dink is a diplomat?"

The green-haired woman stepped forward, symbolically removing herself from Fury's protection. "You don't need that information," she said imperiously.

Wolverine was unimpressed. "And you don't need both those arms, Lettuce Locks."

Fury chose to ignore the direct threat to the green-haired woman. "I'd like some answers myself," he said, pointing toward Colossus. "For starters: Wasn't that guy dead?"

Kitty frowned. *They didn't know? They* had *to know. Is Fury screwing with us now?* "He was here," she said, fighting to keep her anger in check. "Here being tortured. Being tested by Ord like an animal so you could design your cure."

"I don't know what you're talking about," Fury said.

"Oh, right, nobody knows anything," said Kitty. She looked toward Rao. "And you? You still claiming that you were in the dark about that?"

"Absolutely," said Rao. "I would never condone—"

"Your lies are getting less convincing with repetition," said Emma. "Fury, you're clearly in bed with this alien berk, yet you've no clue what he's been up to? Doesn't sound like you, great big covert muckity and all that."

A moment passed.

I would not want to play poker with this man, Emma's thoughts informed the others. *He is seriously brassed off, that much is obvious. But I don't know whether he really doesn't know what's going on, or if he's just irritated that we're on to him.*

So what's his play, thought Wolverine.

He'll probably try an end run. Try to deny—

"How do you know your 'Colossus' is the genuine article in the first place?" said Fury.

And there it is, Emma commented wryly as she said aloud, "I read his mind."

"I matched his DNA," said the Beast.

"I smelled him," said Wolverine.

Beast nodded. "I also did that."

"This," said Kitty forcefully, "is Peter Niko-laievitch Rasputin. And you owe him the goddamn truth."

Fury's expression never changed, never so much as flinched. But there was a growing anger in his single visible eye.

"Agent Brand?" Fury said, very softly, very dangerously.

The green-haired woman turned and looked with irritation at Fury. At least Kitty supposed it was irritation. The glasses made her eyes impossible to read. "You don't have the authorization to make me divulge classified—"

"Yeah? What I *do* got is the urge to disappear and leave this dink," and he inclined his head toward Ord's unconscious form, "at the mercy of these very unreasonable super-powered types. Tell them the truth, Brand. It ain't like they're gonna like it, and it's the only option you got if you want this nimrod alive. Because I'll tell ya what: I dunno for sure that the Commie over there—no offense—"

"None taken, capitalist lackey."

Fury paused. "God, I miss the Cold War," he said wistfully. "Where was I? I dunno if he's got what it takes to off your boy Ord in cold blood. He's pissed now, but from the look of him, I'm thinking he won't, if for no other reason than it'll damage him in the eyes of the little lady over there. Right?" Before Kitty could say anything, he continued, "On the other hand, I've known Wolverine more years than either of us would admit. And Wolverine, well…he'd gut him like a trout without a second thought. Am I right, Logan?"

"Actually, I wouldn't give it a first thought."

Fury gestured toward Emma and Cyclops. "And I wouldn't count on Frosty the Snow Queen to stop him. Laser Gazer might, but—"

"I'm feeling faint," Cyclops said humorlessly. "I could pass out at any time, and God knows *what* could happen while I'm unconscious."

"Right, so…your call, Agent Brand. Make your peace with it, or they'll make their pieces with him."

There was a long moment of silence. Then Brand turned to face the assembled X-Men. "I'm Special

Agent Abigail Brand. I head the Sentient Worlds Observation and Response Department. We work with S.H.I.E.L.D. and handle matters extraterrestrial."

Beast ran the name through his head. "Sentient Worlds Obser—S.W.O.R.D.? And S.H.I.E.L.D. The government and their acronyms...honestly, it's adorable."

"I didn't pick the name." Brand paced back and forth, a couple steps one way, a couple the other, as if she were delivering a briefing—which, to all intents and purposes, she was. "The thing is, S.H.I.E.L.D. has its hands full trying to keep *this* world together. And *somebody* has to keep track of the others."

"So funding terrorists isn't just for earthlings anymore?" Cyclops did not appear impressed by her mission statement. "We selling arms to the Skrulls, too?"

"What we're doing, Mister Summers, is trying to prevent a war. We're—"

"Uh-oh," Wolverine said abruptly, and the hackles went up on the back of the Beast's neck as he growled low in his throat.

"What is it?" said Fury. The rest of the S.H.I.E.L.D. agents looked around, uncertain.

Then they heard the noises. The shouts, the sounds of pounding feet, echoing so it was impossible to be sure where they were coming from.

"Perimeter team, report!" Fury snapped, and waited to hear a response on his ear piece. Nothing came. "Perimeter team, this is Fury! Anything ya care to share with us—?"

Then a mob of rampaging mutants came charging in through the hole that Ord had created when he made his entrance.

"*Where is it! Where's the cure!*" a bizarre grotesque of a mutant was shouting. His face was in his gut and he had no head, and there were more behind him, lots more. "*You can't take it away from us!*"

"*The government!*" another mutant shouted, pointing at Fury. "*The government is going to take the cure away!*"

"*Hold your fire!*" Fury shouted. "These are *civilians!*"

Like a ghostly personification of every mutant who had ever been wronged, a floating blue girl descended on the Beast. He had the strange feeling she was drawn to him because she sensed the uncertainty within him. "No more waiting," she said, her voice airy, seemingly hardly there, as ephemeral as she was herself. "*No more waiting…need body…whole body…need be human.*" The Beast was shaken, as if he'd seen all of his inner concerns and confusions personified in front of him. As if he was being haunted by his own soul.

FURY noticed the X-Men were doing nothing to impede the mutants. Instead the X-Men had flattened against what was left of the walls, trying to stay out of the way, as the mutants overran the S.H.I.E.L.D. agents. It made him wonder if the two groups were in cahoots somehow.

Several mutants converged on Doctor Rao, demanding the cure. "I can't," she cried out. "It isn't fully tested yet!"

Clearly they didn't care. Several of them grabbed Rao, started shaking her. The Beast tried to get to her, but there were too many people between them. S.H.I.E.L.D. agents fired tasers at Rao's assailants; two mutants went down, and then the agents made the mistake of trying to taser a large one with a rocky hide. Not only did the electricity bounce off him, but his large hand stabbed forward, grabbed the nearest gun, and broke it in half—to the shock of the disarmed S.H.I.E.L.D. agent.

Fury found himself surrounded by seven identical dwarfs—apparently one mutant who had replicated six duplicates of himself. None of the dwarfs seemed remotely happy. Fury glanced around, trying to get a line on where the X-Men were. There was no sign of them. They'd slipped away in the chaos.

Then a report crackled over his headset: *"Sir! We've had a perimeter breach on the southwest corner!"*

"Really? That's good to know."

"It's a full scale riot, sir! The mutants who were lined up outside, they attacked when they saw us!

They assumed we—"

"Yeah, I figured it out, Captain Obvious." Call in the Sandmen, put 'em to sleep, and then demote yourself to *crossing guard!*"

THE crush of mutants carried the battle into and down the adjoining corridor. Special Agent Brand was going with the flow, seeing no advantage to slugging it out with a bunch of invading mutants. This was not her problem. Her problem was getting Ord to—

Suddenly she stopped.

She ran back into the lab to make sure Ord had been secured. He'd been lying unconscious on the floor, and she couldn't take the chance that—

Brand skidded to a halt. There was a large dent in the floor where Ord had been. The fight had moved out of the room, and apparently so had Ord.

She ran into the adjoining lab, through the hole in the wall. There was no sign of him. She tapped her headset, but could barely hear herself think over the insanity in the hallway. "We need agents up in research right now! Ord is loose and very unstable—!"

Suddenly she began to sink.

For an instant she thought perhaps she was passing out. Then she realized that, no, she really was sinking, as if the floor had transformed into quicksand. She looked down to see a slender female hand clamped onto her ankle, and she had just enough time to think, *Oh, that little* —before her entire body passed right through the floor.

She was hauled down, down, everything spinning around her so fast that she couldn't get her bearings. Then abruptly she was yanked sideways. In the darkness of passing walls and insubstantial floors, she caught a brief glimpse of Kitty Pryde's back. She was pulling Brand along by the ankle like a balloon in the Macy's Thanksgiving parade.

Then suddenly Brand felt a chill and realized she was outside. She hung in the air for a moment, like the Coyote becoming vulnerable to gravity upon realizing he'd run off the edge of a cliff. Then she materialized, dropped, and landed with a jarring thud on the ground, knocking the wind out of her. Fortunately, the drop was only a couple of feet.

She felt her stomach muscles squeeze and, even though she tried to avoid it, she couldn't. She knelt on her hands and knees and dry-heaved like a drunk, thanking providence she had forgotten to eat that day aside from a couple of protein bars. When the wave of nausea finally passed, she shook it off and looked up.

The X-Men surrounded her. Kitty Pryde, who had led her on the disorienting trip, was looking particularly smug. The dragon she called Lockheed was sitting serenely on her shoulder. The others were staring down at her.

"Hi," said Kitty. "Remember us?"

TWENTY

TILDIE.

It was the only thought going through Kavita Rao's mind as she sprinted through the hallways of Benetech. The sounds of battle, the shouting, all of it receded into the distance. The only thing that mattered was making sure Tildie was all right.

Despite all her efforts to help mutants anxious to leave their disease behind, she had never felt quite so terrified as she had when they stormed Benetech. Their desperation was palpable, and that desperation had flipped over into anger and frustration that was worse than anything she had ever imagined.

I announced it too early. I wanted to give them hope that a cure was coming. So many of them felt no miracle would ever occur…that they'd be trapped in their misshapen states forever and might even end their existence because they could no longer tolerate it...I wanted them to know help was on the horizon. I wanted to save lives. Instead I've driven them into a frenzy with desire for the cure.

I have to keep them away from Tildie. God only knows what they'd do if they found her. What if...what if one of them has some sort of vampiric abilities, and just...just sucks her dry, thinking her blood is the key? Anything could happen if they get to her.

The observation room where Tildie resided at Benetech had a lockdown mode that would turn it into the equivalent of a panic room. But there was no guarantee it had been activated. In fact, it was possible that the X-Men had inadvertently taken it off-line during their entry, which meant it would have to be activated manually by one of the few people in the company who knew the codes.

Such as Rao herself.

The S.H.I.E.L.D. agents had managed to pull her out from under the pileup of mutants surrounding her. "Don't hurt them!" she had said as they extracted her, shoving the mutants to either side.

"Get out of here!" one of the agents had said. "We can't guarantee your safety!"

She had been about to offer protest, but then she thought of Tildie. With that, all other concerns had vanished, and she had sprinted down the hallways, through the corridors, to the observation room.

In her mind's eye, she could see Tildie there, up until all hours as she frequently was. Oftentimes Tildie would have a late-night tea party to entertain her stuffed toys. It was such a pleasant display of normality that it gave Rao hope that someday the child could grow up into a life not haunted by dreams or nightmares. Granted, the reason Tildie often displayed behavior bordering on insomnia was because she tried to put off going to sleep for as long as possible, since the prospect of slumber held its own terrors. Ideally, though, all would be well with her eventually, and this terrible past truly would be past.

As Rao neared the observation room, she was alarmed to hear a thunderous crash and a massive shattering of glass. Instantly she knew what it was. Someone had smashed in the observation window.

She shoved open the door into the observation room and, sure enough, the glass was lying in a million shards. All during the experiments, Tildie had remained blissfully unaware that she was being watched through the window; she'd just thought it to be a big mirror.

Rao could also tell at a quick glance that all the records had been taken. The various file folders, the test results, all of it. The computer screen was blank save for error messages that indicated all the hard drives had been wiped, the files either destroyed or transferred and then deleted.

Rao moved to the large empty space the glass had occupied, and gaped through it in horror.

Ord was in the room with Tildie. The table with her tea party had been knocked over, and Ord was holding Tildie up like a football, with one hand clamped over her mouth. He was so strong that her struggles were utterly futile.

"Put her down!" Rao shouted.

Ord barely afforded her a glance. There was nothing but fury in his face. "If I can't conduct tests on Colossus, then I'll conduct them on her. And if they can't be done here, then they'll be held elsewhere. *Retrieval.*"

The moment he said that last word, a large bracelet on his wrist began to glow. Tildie's eyes were wide with terror. Seconds later, a silvery glow surrounded him and then he was gone, along with Tildie. It was some manner of transport fail-safe.

"Oh God," Rao whispered.

It was as if Tildie's nightmares-made-into-reality had returned, except this time around, the nightmare was not something conjured out of the girl's own head. Instead it was a devil spat up from Hell, and Kavita Rao had made a deal with it.

Rao stared at Tildie's toys, upended and lying in an accusatory fashion on the floor.

Then she turned and bolted.

* * * *

THE X-Men stood a safe distance from the insanity being unleashed upon Benetech, under a grove of trees that blocked them from easy view of low-flying S.H.I.E.L.D. vehicles. Anyone on the ground who happened to glance their way didn't see them; a simple mental deflection from Emma was enough to guarantee that.

In the distance, the X-Men could see masses of mutants still pouring in through the breach they'd created in the side of the building. A half dozen small ships—one-man S.H.I.E.L.D. vessels—were dive-bombing down toward them. The mutants had crashed in through the first floor in the southwest corner and spread throughout the facility in no time at all. Fortunately, the building seemed in no danger of collapsing; otherwise hundreds of people already inside would be crushed.

There was no sign of Nick Fury. Obviously he was still inside the building, although there was little doubt that he was responsible for calling in the air strike.

The newly arrived S.H.I.E.L.D. vessels targeted those mutants who were still trying to gain entry. Huge blasts of gas hammered away at the mob as if the ships were crop dusters. This was far more potent gas than any the X-Men had ever seen before. The moment it hit the ground, anyone within range simply keeled over immediately. No coughing or gasping or staggering; just down they went.

Cyclops' gut impulse was to open fire on the ships, just blast them out of the sky. But the X-Men were hardly in a position to start a full-blown firefight with S.H.I.E.L.D.

For just a moment, as Cyclops watched the desperate mutants being felled by the S.H.I.E.L.D. sleeper ships, he suddenly remembered what it was like to see a world through something other than a ruby-quartz visor. He remembered colors, and the feel of the wind on his face, and having to squint in sunlight. And crying. He remembered crying. He remembered when his eyes had first turned into weapons of mass destruction. If this cure had been around when he'd undergone that transformation, how likely was it that he would have been standing at the front of the line waiting for his dose?

Likely. Damned likely.

The X-Men had always been symbols of what people could accomplish when they were forced to adjust to strange, new abilities. But if there was a new reality where mutants didn't *have* to adjust…

…why should they be *forced* to?

Symbols were all well and good, but all the X-Men were—all they *really* were—were examples of what mutants could be if they chose to live their lives *as* mutants. Rather than allow themselves to be beaten down by society, mutants could band together and create a world where they lived in solidarity with each other and drew strength from that. A strength that would enable them to survive long enough for society to realize that mutants were simply different, not enemies.

But that was only true if there was no alternative. Rao's 'miracle' was providing exactly that, and who were the X-Men…who was *anyone*…to make that decision on behalf of others?

You've known so much misery, so much heartache in your life, with this genetic burden that was thrust upon you. Where do you get off sitting in judgment on other people's pursuit of happiness? You're opposed to the government forcing people to take this cure…but if you're working to deprive people of it when they really want it, how are you any better? In what kind of world do you get to seize the moral high ground?

"A world of trouble. That's what you people are in. A *world* of trouble," said Agent Brand, jolting Cyclops harshly from his mental digression.

His stoicism remained intact. Long years of suppressing emotion enabled him to keep his face impassive. "Well, that's the world we're from," he said drily. "Finish your story, Agent Brand."

Her sunglasses had fallen off when she hit the ground. She hadn't bothered to pick them up, and he noticed her eyes were as green as her hair. "Genocide. *'And they all died suddenly after.* The end.' You like it?"

"My kind of party," said Wolverine.

"Are you remotely under the impression that I'm kidding, little man?" she said. "The Breakworld's technologies include something that translates roughly as 'Timeshadows.' They can see a partial version of the future. Not visit. Not change. Just see."

"And they saw something of interest to us?" said Cyclops.

She nodded. "They saw their world in chaos. In ashes. The Breakworld, gone in their lifetimes. Destroyed utterly. By a mutant. Most probably an X-Man."

Wolverine stepped forward, grabbed her by the front of her uniform and hauled her to her feet. "So you got together and decided to take care of the muties once and for all, huh?"

"Don't you get it? To Ord, *he's* the hero fighting to save his world. You people are the enemy. He's the X-Man to your Magneto."

"Magneto said people will always look for reasons to destroy mutants." Wolverine's fists curled even more tightly around the top of her uniform. "So far you ain't shown me anything to prove he got it wrong."

"Deal with the facts, Bumblebee. Our own precog stats confirmed Ord's findings," said Brand, undaunted by the angry mutant. "A mutant will almost certainly destroy the Breakworld in the next three years."

"And what do we know of this Breakworld?" said Emma. "Have you seen it yourself?"

"No. But it has a quarter of a billion people living on it. It celebrates the arts, scientific discovery, philosophy—"

"And the one representative of this paradise that you've encountered firsthand," the Beast pointed out, "is a bellicose madman who's armed to the teeth. Even allowing for the possibility that what you're saying is true…have you considered the notion that Break-world's alleged destruction will result from their own endeavors? Perhaps they're a race of conquerors that targets Earth and a mutant winds up saving our world…*again*. Did you give any thought to that possibility? Or did your own personal dislike of mutants make it simple for you to decide whose side you're on?"

"My feelings toward mutants, one way or the other, are not at issue," she said stiffly. "Although I'm curious: When your teammate, Jean Grey, went berserk and destroyed an entire alien world a few years back, what rationalization did you come up with to excuse that?"

"Jean Grey is dead, Agent Brand," Emma said, with a sense of finality that indicated that, as far as she was concerned, that subject was closed.

Yet Brand, who smirked at the words, wasn't about to let it go. "Yeah, that'll last," she said and looked toward Peter Rasputin.

Immediately Kitty was between them. Brand flinched slightly; clearly she had no desire to experience the literally gut-wrenching sensation of another Kitty Pryde-sponsored architectural tour. "You have a hell of a nerve," said Kitty sharply, "holding up Peter's resurrection as an example of anything other than your pal Ord's sheer cruelty. Ord brought Peter back to life and then spent God knows how long torturing him. *Ord* is the one using *us* for lab rats. Did you know?" and her voice became accusatory. "Did you know what he was doing to Peter? All this time, did you know? Give me a damned straight answer."

Brand didn't attempt to dissemble. "Yes. But Fury didn't. Not his department."

"What about Kavita?" asked Beast.

"Ord came here with a declaration of *war,* people," said Brand. "The cure was just diplomatic tap dancing until we could get a bead on which mutant was—"

The Beast was not so easily put off. "Please answer my question. In case it's slipped your mind: Was Doctor Rao aware that you were—"

"Please!"

The shouted plea had come from Doctor Rao, sprinting across the lawn toward them. The moment she had their attention, she skidded to a halt. She was gasping for air, her hand to her chest, trying to compose herself. "He's got Tildie," she managed to get out.

"The kid?" said Wolverine. Rao nodded. "And I s'pose we don't gotta ask who the 'he' is."

Again she nodded. "He's taken everything. The samples, the research. He's gone below and I...if Tildie's hurt..."

"Why below?" said Cyclops. "What's below?"

Kitty was able to supply the answer immediately. "A subcomplex. His lab."

Brand had her hand to her ear, activating her comm device. "Fury. It's Brand," she said briskly. "Total evac *now*. Five hundred yard minimum."

Cyclops was starting to feel truly irritated that he kept asking questions without getting any answers. "What's going on? What's he gonna do?"

"He's gonna leave," said Brand tersely.

"The girl's still inside," said Cyclops. He started to move in the direction of the building, with the others following.

Brand stepped into their path. "You won't be able to rescue her if you're dead, and if you don't give this area some distance immediately—"

Abruptly, the ground began to rumble beneath their feet. The X-Men exchanged glances of alarm as Brand started to run. "She's right! Fall back for the moment!" called out Cyclops. Not seeing any other option, the team charged after Brand, reasoning— not incorrectly—that she would know which way to go to avoid whatever was coming.

The Beast, loping along, easily caught up with Brand. *"What's he got under there?!"*

"His ship!" Brand called to him as she continued to sprint. *"There were natural caverns, formations under Benetech! His ship's FTL drive warps space around it, so he was able to land it in there by basically warping right into it!"*

"Why isn't he doing that now?"

"It's ion powered! He needs to build up an energy supply of solar ions to fire up the warp, get it online!"

People poured out of Benetech now, the incredible vibrations causing entire sections of the building to crack apart and fall within. Fury and the other S.H.I.E.L.D. agents emerged, a number of them carrying fallen, unconscious mutants slung over their shoulders or cradled in their arms. Some of the mutants were helping others of their kind, and a few were even carrying downed S.H.I.E.L.D. agents.

Then a vast area of the ground began to pulsate, to bulge, as something subterranean pushed upward from beneath. The quaking continued, increasing in violence until even the most sure-footed of mutants were having trouble remaining upright.

Then the ground exploded, clods of dirt and rock flying upwards. People ducked and shielded their heads from the debris. The sounds of powerful engines were still muffled but growing louder and clearer by the second.

The top of the ship appeared, a dome—the cockpit or bridge—ringed with a series of viewports, and moments later the rest emerged, tearing up the ground, sending tons of dirt scattering in all directions. It was shaped like a pyramid, with twin engines roaring beneath, propelling it skyward.

Fury had drawn near Brand as they watched the ship start to angle toward the heavens.

"You were gonna brief me on this, I'm sure," Fury said with dry annoyance.

She ignored the implied criticism. "Can you bring him down?"

"With what we have on hand? Not a chance."

"He's got the bloody serum, people!" said Emma, sensing an opportunity. "We hit him with the jet and blow it all to smoking pieces—him, the research and the 'cure.'"

"There's a girl in there with him," Kitty reminded her.

Doctor Rao said, "You have to help her—!"

"Thoughts, people?" said Beast. "Because I'm thinking another ten seconds and he and the girl are gone."

"No." It was Colossus, his voice rumbling like thunder. "He doesn't get away with this, and with her." Then he looked to Wolverine, and immediately it was obvious to all that the two of them were on the same wavelength.

"You feeling rested up, Petey?"

"I am strong."

Wolverine nodded. It was all he needed to hear. "If that's the case, then I got just two words for you, bub."

"Fastball special?" said Colossus.

"Just like old times."

Instantly the metal sheathing that was Peter's greatest offensive and defensive weapon slid into place. Seconds later, the armor-clad mutant picked up Wolverine, who flattened out his body, arms forward like a swimmer caught in mid-racing dive. Or, more accurately, like a human javelin. The "fastball special" was the first combined combat tactic that the two of them had ever developed. "Oldie but goodie," murmured Wolverine, and then Colossus drew back his arm slightly and hurled Wolverine skyward.

"You really *have* kept in shape," Emma said with admiration and even a bit of contemplation.

Colossus' aim could not have been more perfect.

Cyclops and the others watched as Wolverine speared upward, his arms outstretched, his claws extended. The ship started to build up speed. For a moment it looked as if the acceleration was going to cause Wolverine to miss it clean, which would result in a very frustrating and bruising landing. But Wolverine had just enough speed to bang into the side of the ship. He jammed the claws of his right hand into the hull and dangled there for a moment, getting his bearings.

But Wolverine was hardly safe. Indeed, he was in greater jeopardy than ever. The ship was still heading toward space, perhaps even a jump into some sort of faster-than-light warp. Any sane person would realize he was overmatched. Any sane person would cut his losses, release his hold on the ship, and go into free-fall, trusting his natural healing power to kick in and manage to repair his broken body after landing.

But none of that really applied to Wolverine, because he was the best there was at what he did.

And what he did was act totally insane. Especially when it came to children being threatened and kidnapped.

So he brought his left arm around, shoved those claws into the ship's hull, and started pulling himself arm over arm over the top of the ship, toward the viewing ports and cockpit. Because Wolverine would rather end up as a suffocated, shriveled corpse floating somewhere in the depths of space, than give up.

TILDIE sat crouched in the far corner of the ship's bridge, bathed in pale red light. She kept whispering the same thing, over and over: "Wanna wake up now. Wanna wake up now."

"Is that what you think?" said Ord, seated at the controls. He was watching with relief as the ground receded far below him. "That you're sleeping? Dreaming? Having a waking nightmare? How utterly amusing."

The plan had seemed simplicity itself: Ord would, in conjunction with the human scientists, finish research on the cure and administer it to Earth's mutant population. Getting rid of all their powers would effectively "neuter" them so they would provide no threat to the BreakWorld. Meanwhile Ord himself would destroy the more determined and organized mutants, such as the X-Men, either with the cure—as he had with that annoying flying boy—or through simple brute strength.

But matters had not gone exactly according to plan. The X-Men had proven far too unwilling to die, and now his alliance with Agent Brand had been revealed. That annoying Nick Fury—about whom Brand had had very little positive to say other than that, "If Fury finds out about this we are positively screwed"—knew everything about their activities.

But all was not a total loss, thanks to his acquisition of the sobbing girl behind him. She was a bargaining chip, one that would prove useful in dealing with the Earth people. In that respect, Ord had caught a lucky break. There were very few races in the galaxy whose members would willingly give up an advantage, or hesitate to take action, for the life of a single miserable child. Yet that was what Ord had stumbled upon.

"Did the Doctor tell you there would be no more nightmares, little one?" he said in a conversational tone. He glanced backward and saw her give the slightest, timid nod. "Did you always know she was lying?"

Once again a tiny nod. Good. The girl had more brains than he'd credited her with.

"Good. Because there *will* be nightmares," he assured her. "I will make the Earth an endless, shrieking blackness." He smiled then, and fortunately his back was to her because his smile was a terrible thing to see, and Tildie already had enough nightmarish images to live with. "They probably think I'm returning to my homeworld, but they could not be more wrong. There are other places on this world where I can safely hide and wait for my opportunity. And the first thing I will attend to, once they have forgotten about me, is the mutants. I have my 'cure' now, and as long as I have you, they'll wait just long enough for me to—"

The viewing port directly in front of Ord shattered and a curled fist stabbed forward with the speed and ferocity of a serpent. Ord cried out in alarm. It was an involuntary reaction, but it cost him dearly as the fist plunged deep inside his mouth.

Wolverine extended his upper torso into the cockpit, snarling upside down into Ord's face. His fist pressed against the back of Ord's mouth. "You bite, I'll heal. I pop my claws, you won't. *Land.*"

Ord took a moment, then grunted his acquiescence. He reversed the thruster, and in a slow, graceful arc the ship started to angle back toward Benetech.

"That's it. Thaaaat's it," said Wolverine. "Nice and easy on the controls there. We all want a smooth landing, don't we?" Ord grunted again and Wolverine raised his voice slightly. "Tildie? You still with me over there, kid? He didn't hurt you none, did he?" The child made no answer, her eyes wide with terror. "You got nothing to be afraid of, kid. I know I look scary, but I'm one of the good guys—"

Then Ord hit the braking thrusters.

It was only a momentary diversion, but it was all Ord required. The thrusters fired in reverse, bringing the ship to the equivalent of a panic stop in midair. Tildie screamed and slid from the back of the cockpit to the front, thudding painfully against the underside of the console. Because Ord was belted in tightly and prepared, he was able to keep himself upright and back against the seat.

As for Wolverine, there were many rules that he was capable of ignoring, but the laws of physics were not among them. Objects in motion tended to stay in motion, and the violent stop propelled him forward, forcing his hand out of Ord's mouth. His claws popped out a second too late to be of any use. An instant later, he was gone, propelled through the window and out of the ship.

"Hah!" shouted Ord. He looked out the shattered

window and saw no sign of Wolverine. At the speed the mutant had been moving, he'd probably already hit the ground by now.

They were just above Benetech, and Ord could see the frustrated mutants helpless upon the ground. The last they would see of him would be the rear of his departing vessel, and they would know that—

Something sliced across his forearm in a blur, and he screamed in pain. For a moment he thought it was Wolverine back from the dead, but he was wrong.

Ord, as it turned out, had not been completely immune to the effects of the sudden deceleration. He hadn't realized that his spiked-ring weapon had come free of its holster and lodged under the control panel.

Tildie had extracted it.

She was standing not two feet away from him, gripping the weapon with both hands. She was neither trembling nor in panic. Holding a weapon seemed to give her some degree of confidence, a sense of control.

"No more nightmares," she whispered.

"Put that down," said Ord, "before you hurt yourself."

He tried to grab the weapon, and she whipped it around. There was no artistry or combat style to her assault. But considering even a glancing blow could cut through his armor and to the bone, she didn't have to be precise. If Ord had yanked his arm back a second later, she would have hacked off his hand.

This was insane. He had dispatched the X-Men with little to no difficulty, and he was being held at bay by a frantic child?

"Give me that!" he roared, yanking clear his straps.

*"**No more nightmares!**"* she screamed, right back at him. She came at him, swinging the vicious weapon back and forth like a scythe.

Ord backed up across the cockpit, slowly, trying to time Tildie's swings. When he was sure he had it down, he swung a fast kick toward her. His timing was perfect, catching her on the downswing, and it knocked her on her side. She cried out, losing her grip on his weapon, and it clattered across the floor. He started to reach for it.

And that was when he lost control of the ship.

WOLVERINE tumbled out the port window, cursing himself profusely for allowing himself to be distracted by the girl. Except it wasn't really her fault; there was no point in blaming anyone but himself.

With a miles-long drop yawning beneath him, Wolverine twisted in midair in a movement that by any reasonable measure should have been impossible. He managed to sink his claws into the hull once more, but the ship was tilted nose-up, and this time he slid down the middle of the hull lengthwise. His claws gutted it like a trout, but the toes of his boots glanced helplessly off the slick surface. He couldn't stop his downward slide.

He realized he was heading straight toward one of the thrusters. Powerful blasts of energy streamed out of it, keeping the ship in place in midair. Fortunately, thanks to the design of the ship, there was a ledge right above the thruster. Wolverine slid right toward the ledge and seconds later, his feet were braced against it.

Quickly, he sliced into the ship's hull, effectively creating his own hatchway. The thruster roared all around him, nearly deafening, and there was an aroma of concentrated ozone, as if he were scrambling around within the center of a lightning storm. He eased his way into the very guts of the ship, cramped into a narrow utilities tube that was a latticework of circuitry and energy relays.

Wolverine wasn't an engineer or an expert in alien technology.

He was, however, extremely expert in being the monkey wrench in the works.

He started hacking away with his claws, accomplishing two things simultaneously: disrupting the energy flow through the circuitry, and carving himself a way into the vessel's interior.

It took him only seconds to cut through what

turned out to be the ceiling of a hallway, which he dropped into feet first. The ship was shuddering all around him. He could actually hear the mighty thrusters choking, practically eating themselves, as the energy relays tried to reroute themselves and failed. Knowing which direction the cockpit lay, he sprinted along the hallway, which was starting to tilt downward. The angle wasn't sharp at first, but it was increasing dramatically.

He was running out of time.

ORD fell backwards against the ship's controls, trying to steady himself. He managed to reach down, pick up his ringed weapon and fasten it back into place. Tildie cowered a short distance away, but he couldn't be bothered with her; he would hack her to pieces later.

He didn't understand the readings he was seeing. Energy wasn't getting to the engines. The ship was sputtering, dying.

Had he been in space, he would simply have shut down the engines and allowed the ship to drift while he sorted things out. But that wasn't an option here. Gravity was having its say, and as the last of the ship's thrusting capacity began to choke out, his vessel was displaying as much maneuverability as a dying pig.

Suddenly Tildie started thudding bare fists on his

arm. "Get away!" he shouted at her and knocked her aside as he worked desperately to coax energy out of the engines.

Suddenly, there was the sound of tearing metal behind him. Ord risked a glance around. To his shock, Wolverine had just hacked his way through the far door of the bridge. The mutant sprinted across the deck, snarled, "Need some help with the controls?" and jammed his claws deep into the console. He ripped it open, sparks flying everywhere including into Ord's face. Little bits of the alien's flesh ignited, and he cried out as he batted at them.

The engines died completely. And suddenly, just like that, the ship was in free-fall.

TILDIE shrieked in terror, and Wolverine ran to her. She was in total panic mode, and Wolverine couldn't blame her. He didn't have time to tap-dance with her, however.

"Trust me," he shouted, knowing she had no reason to, hoping that she would.

With a roar, Ord lunged at them. Wolverine darted to one side, and a backslash of his claws caught Ord along his ribcage. Ord let out a howl of pain. It wasn't quite the full payback Wolverine would have liked, but it was the closest he was going to manage.

Wolverine had no idea how close they were to the

ground. He would do everything he could to shield Tildie from the impact, but he was concerned it wouldn't be enough.

He charged toward the shattered window and leaped through it with all the strength in his powerful legs. Moments later, the ship was falling in one direction and Wolverine—with Tildie clutched to him—the other. Then Wolverine saw how far down the ground was and realized he'd misjudged badly. He would survive; it'd hurt like hell, but he'd survive. But the impact would be too much for the child. Even with his body wrapped around her, her bones would shatter on impact.

They fell, end over end, Wolverine curled in a protective circle. *Emma…if you're listening…a little help. A small miracle. If that ain't too much of a problem…*

Get ready, came back a sharp reply.

Ready? Ready for wh—?

Suddenly something banged up against them in midair.

"What the hell!" said Wolverine.

Against the rushing noise of the air, he heard the last thing he expected: Kitty Pryde saying, *"Hold onto her! Get ready!"* Sure enough, Kitty's arms were wrapped around them.

"Ready for what?"

Wolverine, Kitty, and Tildie hit the ground together, and then dropped straight through it. Their momentum continued to carry them down, down, into darkness and dirt, where it was impossible to see anything. Even Wolverine felt creeped out by the sensation of premature burial.

Then, suddenly, their downward plummet reversed itself. They floated upward, slowly but steadily. Wolverine had Tildie pressed against him, her face buried in his chest so she wouldn't see what was happening around them.

Seconds later they broke the surface, coming up from underground, to the delight and relief of the other X-Men. Kitty staggered a little once they materialized. She sagged against Colossus, who caught her. "Don't ever tell me to do that again," Colossus said to her in a voice filled with relief.

Then Wolverine understood. Colossus had performed a fastball special with Kitty Pryde, hurling her the same way that he had thrown Wolverine. Except this had been even more of a challenge. With Wolverine, Colossus had been aiming at an entire ship. In this case, he had slung Kitty directly at the falling Wolverine and Tildie. If his timing and aim had been anything less than precise, Kitty would have gone flying right past them. Instead she had managed to snag them in midair, accomplishing the miracle that Wolverine had hoped for, but not really expected.

"*Tildie!*"

The child had been shivering, sobbing in Wolverine's grasp, but then she heard her name shouted by the one voice in the world she trusted. Immediately she uncurled herself from Wolverine and, stumbling to her feet, sprinted toward Doctor Kavita Rao. Tildie practically leaped into her arms, and Rao hugged her tightly, like a gratified mother.

Then Wolverine noticed that events had not stopped while he was underground.

About two hundred yards away, the remains of Ord's ship were a massive crumbled heap upon the ground. Smoke rose from all over, and S.H.I.E.L.D. agents were dousing the wreckage with foam to put out little fires. Other agents swarmed all over the ship, examining it.

"Looks like I missed the big event," said Wolverine.

"Yeah. Talk about your close encounters," Kitty said. She smiled wanly, clearly exhausted. "Is Ord dead?"

"With any luck," said Colossus grimly. "With any luck he is."

THEY had no luck.

Ord, as it turned out, was still alive. He was unconscious when they found him. By the time he came around, he had been solidly encased in electronic braces that ran across his chest and legs, immobilizing them. He snarled, he struggled, but he was helpless to budge them. It brought Cyclops some measure of satisfaction to see a group of S.H.I.E.L.D. agents lugging Ord along, suspended between two lines of agents via a sling, like a cooked hog being hauled to a luau.

Fury stood there, watching Ord being taken away, with the rest of the X-Men nearby. Kavita was keeping Tildie close, and Tildie didn't seem inclined to move away from her.

Beast drew near Kavita. She couldn't meet his gaze. In a low voice, the Beast said, "I never received an answer to my question. I would appreciate the courtesy of your honesty. Did you know—?"

"About your man? About Colossus? About his status and what was happening to him?"

He nodded.

She closed her eyes, and all she could say was, "The truth, Henry? The truth is...I didn't ask."

"And he didn't tell."

She nodded.

"That," he said to her, "is quite possibly the worst answer you could have given."

"Henry..."

"Don't say anything more, please."

She nodded again, looked down at the trembling Tildie, and hugged her tight.

* * * *

NICK Fury surveyed the assemblage in front of him. Hands on his hips, he said, "Okay, here's what we're gonna do: not a solitary thing. We all walk away from this like nothing happened—which, after S.H.I.E.L.D. gets done here, will be more or less the truth."

"You are, of course, joking," said Beast.

"Of course," Fury said laconically. "This is one of those jokes I'm so famous and beloved for."

Cyclops faced the S.H.I.E.L.D. director. "What Agent Brand has done is inhumane, illegal, and appalling."

"Yeah, she's a pip," said the S.H.I.E.L.D. director.

"Fury—"

Fury didn't bother to let Cyclops keep talking. "I'm not gonna speak for my counterpart here..."

"I don't—" Brand started to say.

"And neither is she," Fury said sharply. Brand took the hint and her mouth snapped shut. "Fact is, she blew it on many levels, and that will not go... unremarked."

This comment clearly infuriated Brand. She kept her silence in Fury's presence, but her face went remarkably pale except for two spots of red flush on her cheeks.

Fury continued, "But she's dealing with a much bigger picture than any of us. She's trying to stop a war with the Breakworld, a war that just got that much closer to inevitable. And since the only things that got wrecked in that landing," and he nodded toward the mass of twisted metal, "were Doctor Rao's work and the illustrious ambassador, I'd count my blessings and go."

"And that's it?" said Wolverine.

"Yeah, Shortie. That's it."

Cyclops stepped forward. "No apologies, then? No acknowledgment that if you'd been more forthcoming with me in the first place, all of this could have been avoided? When are you going to realize that we're on the same side?"

"Don't kid yourself, Summers. I'm on my side. You're on your side. Sometimes those sides are gonna overlap, and sometimes they ain't. This time out, we had a little of both. Next time it could be more, or maybe less. But I ain't gonna apologize for doing what I had to do. I can, however, give you some advice: In the future, stay out of my way."

"Right back at'cha," said Wolverine.

Fury stared at them for a time, and then shook his head and walked away.

TWENTY-ONE

"**OUR** blessings."

It was the next day, and Scott and Hank were dressed in street clothes, walking the corridors of the school. But Scott was still seething over what he believed to be Nick Fury's high-handed attitude. "Our *blessings?* What blessings would he suggest we count? In causing that crash, Logan destroyed a lot of Rao's work, but that's a setback at most. The cure will be out there, in the hands of government agencies we can't possibly trust."

Hank was in full commiseration with his longtime friend and teammate. "Meanwhile we have mutant riots brewing in every major city over this cure. A student of ours has been neutered by it. And—oh yes!—one of us is predestined to destroy a planet and start an intergalactic war. I'll be blessed."

They stopped at a bay window. From there they had a clear view of two small figures standing outside, one significantly smaller than the other. "We got Pete back," said Scott, gazing out at Peter and Kitty standing a short distance away on a hillock.

"Hell of a thing," said Hank. "Boy's named 'Rasputin.' Should have known he wouldn't be that easy to kill."

There was something else to be said between the two of them. Hank stared sideways at Scott, waiting for him to bring it up. Finally Scott did.

"The cure. Your sample's still cooling in the—"

"I know," said Hank. Anticipating Scott's next question, he continued, "I don't know. I heard about the cure, and it was like this great weight had been lifted from my shoulders. I never felt that weight until I felt it gone. If Ord had tapped me instead of that poor kid, Tildie…maybe this would all be simple. But it's not. I've seen so much self-loathing. These desperate people…"

"I was wrong."

Hank looked at Scott in confusion. "I'm sorry?"

"No, I should be the one apologizing to you," said Scott. "I was being selfish. The fact is that I was more concerned about the prospect of losing you from the team than I was about what was right for you. And for them."

"Them. You mean those mutants who rioted at Benetech."

"Those *people* who rioted. I think that's what we may have been losing track of. They're people, first and foremost, and they're not thinking about the survival of the mutant race, or squaring off against super-powered enemies. They're just trying to get through the day, live their lives. And I don't think I have the right to pass judgment on their decisions just because they don't fall in line with my priorities. I should never have agreed with Logan."

"Actually, Logan was right."

Cyclops stared at him from behind his visor. "This is payback, isn't it? You're saying Logan was right just to irritate me."

"No, he was right….and I'm counting on you never to tell him I said that. Logan said that an X-Man doesn't quit. Not with the world watching."

Cyclops nodded. Then he said, "And if we ever reach a point where mutants have become so accepted that the world *isn't* watching?"

Hank opened the door to his lab. "I'm not saying 'never.'"

"Didn't ask you to." Once again, Scott Summers felt the stirring of his tragedy-filled inner child. But he wasn't ready to think about that. So all he said to Hank was, "So…Pete."

"Hell of a thing," said Hank.

* * * *

WING sat alone in the boys' dormitory. The room was empty. It was a Saturday, no classes, and everyone was off doing things.

Wing was sure that he made everyone feel weird. Ord had chosen Edward for the "demonstration" totally at random. Any of them could have been robbed of their powers. It was pure bad luck that Eddie had been the chosen one.

Even Hisako was steering clear of him, mostly because he had practically torn her head off verbally, telling her to get the hell away from him, saying harshly that he hadn't the slightest interest in anything she had to say. Apparently the message had gotten through loud and clear. He'd managed to chase away everyone who cared about him.

Good job, Eddie, he thought grimly.

There was a soft footfall behind him and, even worse, a rustle of wings. He didn't even have to look to see who it was.

Jay Guthrie...Icarus...stood framed in the doorway. The room was dark, which was unsurprising since Eddie had closed the curtains and shut off the light.

"Here to gloat?" said Eddie.

"Why the hell would I gloat?"

Eddie kept his back fixedly to him. "Because you won. Because I hauled off and punched you, and now I'm nothing. You can fly and I'm stuck here. I'm not

Wing anymore, but you still get to be Icarus, which is, by the way, a stupid name. Icarus flew too close to the sun and got his wings burned off. And he fell to Earth."

"Technically he fell into the sea…"

"Shut up," said Eddie testily. "Point is, I should be Icarus. I should be the one who fell and died. You should be the other guy…"

"Daedalus? His father?"

"Right, him. Exactly."

"I'll think about it."

Jay walked around the end of the bed and went to the window. Before Eddie could stop him, Jay shoved the drapes aside, allowing sunlight to fill the room like something cleansing. Eddie winced and put up a hand to protect his face.

"First of all, I'm not happy about this at all," said Jay. "How can I feel like I won anything when we've lost one of our own? Any diminishment in the ranks affects us all. Miss Pryde said something about it in class, something about islands and bells tolling and stuff like that. Didn't understand it all, but I think it was kind of about this. And second, there's no saying for sure this is permanent."

"It is."

"We don't know that," Jay said firmly. "Even the big brains in government haven't figured out all the ramifications of this 'cure' thing. Something that can be done can be undone."

"There's no hope. I'm never going to fly again."

"Bet'cha you're wrong."

"How would you know?"

"Because I only bet on sure things. You wanna fly?"

"Well yeah. D-uh," he said impatiently.

"All right then." He pushed open the window. The pleasant morning breeze wafted gently into the room. Jay put one foot up on the windowsill and extended a hand toward Eddie. "Let's go."

"It's not the same thing, and you know it."

"Think of it as a down payment on your being cured of the cure."

Eddie wanted to tell him to buzz off. But the call of the sky, the temptation, was too strong.

He reached out to Jay.

Moments later, Icarus was airborne, his arms crisscrossed over Eddie's chest, keeping a firm grip on his friend. His wings carried them higher and higher, and the two young men soared across the sky, free of worries or cares or cures, free of anything save for the urge to fly.

Peter stands next to me, big and warm and muscular and alive. Part of me still wonders if this is all some sort of glorious dream, because it seems too good to be true.

"I leave the world in terrible turmoil," Peter says in his accented English. "I come back. Same turmoil. Nothing different. Well…outfits are a little different." He turns to look at me with those gorgeous blue eyes. "It is funny that it was you who found me, don't you think?"

"No," I say. "I don't think it's funny. I think maybe it's important. I think it's…somehow…I think it's why I'm here."

My small hands disappear into his huge ones.

I can feel my heart pounding in my chest.

I am no longer alone.

The End